Winning The Battle for Your Soul

Overcoming Inner Struggles and Walking in Healing, Hope, and Freedom

Prophetess Dr. Racheal Odoy

Giant Publishing Company
Post Office Box 6455
Lincoln, NE 68506
www.giantpublishingcompany.com

Printed in the United States of America.

Scripture quotations are from the Holy Bible. Scripture references, where used, are for inspirational and educational purposes.

ISBN: 979-8-9898098-8-2
Odoy, Racheal

Winning the Battle for Your Soul
Non-fiction/Racheal Odoy

1. Non-fiction - Christianity
2. Christian living
3. Self-help

Cover design: Prophetess Dr. Racheal Odoy

This book is intended to provide spiritual encouragement and inspiration. It is not intended to replace professional medical, psychological, or counseling advice. Readers experiencing severe emotional or mental distress are encouraged to seek assistance from qualified professionals.

Also by Prophetess Dr. Racheal Odoy:

You Need a Jonathan
Copyright 2018

I and My Seed will Thrive
Copyright 2019

You Have No Carbon Copy
Copyright 2020

Arise, Woman of Light
Copyright 2025

The Kiss of Death
Copyright 2025

The Power of the Mirror
Copyright 2026

The Devil's Label
Copyright 2026

DEDICATION

This book is dedicated to every person who has ever fought a silent battle within their soul.

To those who have wrestled with discouragement, rejection, loneliness, or thoughts that felt too heavy to carry alone—this message is for you.

May these pages remind you that your story is not over. No matter how dark the night may seem, God's light still shines, and hope is never beyond reach.

A Blessing for the Journey

May the words within these pages bring encouragement to your heart and clarity to your mind. May you discover renewed strength for the battles you face and the courage to continue moving forward with faith.

May your thoughts be filled with truth, your heart strengthened with hope, and your spirit renewed with peace.

As you walk this journey, may you remember that no struggle is beyond God's power to heal, restore, and transform.

"The Lord bless you and keep you; the Lord make His face shine upon you and be gracious to you; the Lord turn His face toward you and give you peace." — Numbers 6:24–26

Acknowledgments

I am deeply grateful to God for the grace and inspiration that made this book possible. Every word written in these pages was born from a desire to see lives restored, hearts healed, and souls strengthened.

I also extend heartfelt gratitude to the many people whose encouragement, prayers, and support have made this journey meaningful. Your faith and kindness have been a constant reminder that we were never meant to walk this path alone.

To every reader who holds this book in their hands, thank you for allowing these words to become part of your journey toward healing, hope, and freedom.

FOREWORD

There are moments in life when the greatest battles we face are not visible to the world around us. They are battles within the mind, the heart, and the soul.

Many people appear strong on the outside while quietly fighting internal struggles that few others can see. Feelings of rejection, loneliness, shame, discouragement, and spiritual exhaustion often become burdens carried in silence.

In *Winning the Battle for Your Soul*, Dr. Racheal Odoy invites readers on a journey of understanding, healing, and spiritual renewal. With compassion and biblical insight, she reveals how the enemy seeks to weaken the soul through lies and discouragement, while also offering powerful spiritual principles that lead to restoration and freedom.

This book speaks to anyone who has ever felt overwhelmed by life's challenges or questioned their own worth and purpose. It reminds readers that no matter how deep the struggle may feel, hope and healing are always possible.

The pages that follow are an invitation to rediscover faith, embrace truth, and walk toward a new beginning.

Poem

The Battle Within

There are battles no one sees,
Fought quietly in the depths of the soul.
No armor shines, no swords are drawn,
Yet the struggle can feel just as real.

Some days the mind becomes a battlefield,
Where doubt whispers louder than hope,
Where yesterday's wounds try to speak
Into the possibilities of tomorrow.

But even in the quiet of these battles,
A greater truth remains.
The heart was never meant to surrender
To fear, discouragement, or despair.

Within every soul lies a strength
That cannot be measured by circumstance.
A strength renewed through faith,
Guided by wisdom, and sustained by hope.

For every night that feels heavy
Carries the promise of morning.
And every soul that chooses courage
Begins the journey toward healing.

The battle within may be real,
But it is not the end of the story.
Because every heart that seeks truth
Can discover freedom.
And every life that chooses faith
Can begin again.

Introduction

The Silent Battle Many People Are Fighting

There are battles that people can see, and there are battles that remain hidden deep within the soul.

Every day, countless individuals move through life carrying burdens that others cannot see. They fulfill responsibilities, meet expectations, and interact with the world around them, yet inside they may be wrestling with thoughts and emotions that feel overwhelming.

Some struggle with deep feelings of rejection. Others battle discouragement after painful experiences. Many wrestle with loneliness, comparison, or the quiet voice of self-condemnation that reminds them of past mistakes. There are also those who feel invisible, as though their lives and struggles go unnoticed by the world. These internal battles can slowly drain hope and weaken the spirit.

Behind many of these struggles lies an unseen spiritual conflict. The enemy often seeks to influence the mind and heart by planting seeds of fear, doubt, and despair. Over time, these thoughts can grow into beliefs that shape how people see themselves and how they approach their future.

Yet those thoughts are not the truth.

Scripture reminds us that the battle for the soul is real, but it is not a battle we are meant to fight alone. Throughout the Bible, many individuals faced moments of deep discouragement and spiritual conflict. Even those who walked closely with God experienced seasons when their faith was tested and their strength felt limited. What makes their stories powerful is not the presence of struggle, but the presence of God's restoration.

This book was written for anyone who has ever felt overwhelmed by life's challenges or burdened by internal battles that seem difficult to overcome. It is for those who long for healing, renewed hope, and a deeper understanding of how to silence the voices that attempt to weaken the soul.

Within these pages, you will discover how the enemy often attacks through thoughts of condemnation, rejection, comparison, and despair. At the same time, you will learn the spiritual principles that bring strength, restoration, and freedom.

Prayer, faith, worship, obedience, community, and truth are powerful tools that help restore the soul and renew the mind.

This journey is not about perfection. It is about transformation.

No matter what you have faced in the past, a new beginning is possible. Healing can take place.

Strength can be restored. The voice of the enemy can be silenced.

The battle for your soul may be real, but victory is also real. And the journey toward that victory begins now.

"Your struggles may shape your story, but they do not have the power to define your future."

Table of Contents

Part II

Part III

Closing Sections

Part I
Understanding the Enemy's Attacks

Before a battle can be won, it must first be understood.

Many people spend years fighting emotional and spiritual struggles without fully understanding where the battle is truly coming from. They feel the pain, the confusion, and the heaviness within their hearts, yet they cannot explain why these struggles continue to appear in their lives.

The enemy often works quietly and subtly. Rarely does he appear in obvious ways. Instead, he seeks to influence thoughts, emotions, and perceptions. He whispers lies that slowly shape how people view themselves, their circumstances, and even their relationship with God.

Over time, those whispers can grow into powerful strongholds within the mind and heart.

What begins as a simple thought can eventually develop into a deeply rooted belief. A painful experience can become a lasting wound. Words spoken by others may shape how a person sees their worth and identity.

If these wounds remain unhealed and these lies are not challenged, they can quietly begin to influence the direction of a person's life.

Many people unknowingly begin to live according to the enemy's narrative rather than God's truth. They may start believing they are not worthy, not capable, or not loved. Discouragement becomes familiar, and hopelessness begins to feel like the expected future.

Yet the enemy's greatest weapon is deception. He thrives in darkness, confusion, and silence. When his strategies remain hidden, his influence can grow stronger. But the moment those tactics are exposed, his power begins to weaken. Understanding the enemy's methods is the first step toward defeating them.

In this section, we will explore some of the most common ways the enemy attacks the soul. These attacks often begin quietly but can grow into powerful emotional and spiritual struggles if left unchallenged. By recognizing these patterns, readers will begin to see their struggles with greater clarity. What once felt confusing will begin to make sense. What once felt overwhelming will begin to feel conquerable.

Victory begins with awareness.

Chapter 1
The Invisible Battle Within

Many of the most intense battles people face are the ones no one else can see.

A person may appear calm and composed on the outside while, internally, they are fighting thoughts that refuse to be quiet. They may smile in conversations, fulfill responsibilities, and move through daily routines while privately carrying emotional and spiritual burdens that feel overwhelming. These are the invisible battles of the soul.

Unlike physical struggles, internal battles often go unnoticed. Friends, family members, and coworkers may not recognize the silent conflicts taking place within someone's heart and mind. Yet for the person experiencing them, the struggle can feel relentless.

The Battles No One Sees

Many people carry wounds that others never notice. A painful rejection, a betrayal, a disappointment, or harsh words spoken in anger can remain in the heart long after the moment has passed. Over time, these experiences can quietly shape the way a person sees themselves. Some begin to believe they are not good enough. Others start to feel invisible, as though their lives and struggles do not matter.

These thoughts may seem small at first, but when they repeat often enough, they begin to shape identity. The enemy understands this process very well.

If he can influence what a person believes about themselves, he can influence how they live their life.

How Negative Thoughts Take Root

Spiritual attacks often begin with thoughts. A single negative thought may not seem dangerous, but when it repeats over time, it can slowly grow into a belief. That belief may begin to influence emotions, decisions, and confidence. Someone who repeatedly hears the internal message *"I am not enough"* may eventually accept it as truth. Someone who constantly compares their life to others may begin to feel that their own journey has little value.

This is how the enemy slowly weakens the soul—through repeated lies that shape perception. Yet Scripture reminds us that not every voice we hear within our thoughts reflects truth.

"For God has not given us a spirit of fear, but of power and of love and of a sound mind." — 2 Timothy 1:7

When fear and hopelessness dominate the mind, they often reveal that another voice is attempting to influence the heart.

When Even the Strong Feel Weak

The Bible reveals that even faithful servants of God experienced moments of deep discouragement.

One powerful example is the prophet Elijah. Elijah had witnessed extraordinary miracles. He had seen God move with power and authority. Yet shortly after one of his greatest victories, Elijah found himself overwhelmed by fear and exhaustion.

The same prophet who had stood boldly before powerful opponents suddenly felt alone and defeated. He fled into the wilderness and expressed deep despair. In that moment, the weight of emotional and spiritual exhaustion felt unbearable.

Yet God's response to Elijah is deeply revealing. Instead of condemning him, God restored him. God allowed Elijah to rest. He provided nourishment and spoke to him with gentle guidance that renewed his strength.

This moment reminds us of a powerful truth: Even strong people can experience seasons of deep internal struggle.

Spiritual battles do not mean that faith has failed. Sometimes they simply reveal that the soul is weary and in need of restoration.

When God Restores the Weary Soul

Many people today feel a similar exhaustion. They may be carrying responsibilities, disappointments, and emotional wounds that others cannot see. The weight of these struggles can make life feel overwhelming. Yet the story of Elijah reminds us that God does not abandon those who feel weary.

God restores. He strengthens those who feel weak. He comforts those who feel alone. He renews hope in hearts that have begun to lose their sense of direction. Scripture reminds us: *"Come to me, all you who are weary and burdened, and I will give you rest."* — Matthew 11:28

This invitation reveals God's heart toward those who are struggling. Healing often begins when people recognize that they are not meant to fight these battles alone.

A Truth to Remember

The invisible battles of the soul may feel overwhelming, but they are not permanent.

The enemy may attempt to influence thoughts and emotions, but his voice does not have the final authority. Truth has the power to silence lies. Once the enemy's strategies are recognized, it becomes possible to resist them and walk toward healing and freedom. The battle may be invisible, but victory is real.

Reflection and Prayer

If you have been fighting silent battles within your soul, know that you are not alone.

God sees the struggles that others cannot see. He understands the weight you have been carrying and the questions that may be resting in your heart. Take a moment to reflect on this truth: Your struggles do not define your identity. God's truth has the power to restore what discouragement has tried to weaken.

Prayer

Lord, you see every battle taking place within my heart and mind. You understand the struggles that I sometimes cannot explain. Help me recognize the voices that do not come from you, and give me the strength to stand on your truth. Restore my soul, renew my hope, and guide me toward healing and freedom. Amen.

Chapter 2
The Voice of Condemnation and Self-Hate

There are voices that encourage and strengthen the human spirit, and there are voices that slowly weaken it. One of the most destructive voices a person can hear is the voice of condemnation.

Condemnation is not always loud or obvious. Often it speaks quietly within the mind, repeating accusations about past mistakes, failures, or weaknesses. Over time, these accusations can begin to shape the way a person sees themselves.

Some people live for years carrying the weight of things they regret. They replay painful memories in their minds and wonder if they could have done something differently. Others feel trapped by choices they made long ago and believe that those moments will forever define their future. When these thoughts repeat often enough, they can create deep feelings of shame and self-hatred.

The enemy understands the power of condemnation. If he can convince a person that they are permanently defined by their past, he can keep them from believing in the possibility of change, healing, and restoration.

Condemnation seeks to trap people in a prison built from their own memories. Yet the message of Scripture reveals a very different truth. God does not define people by the worst moment of their lives.

When the Past Becomes a Prison

Many people carry invisible burdens from their past. Some remember mistakes they wish they could erase. Others carry guilt from decisions that brought pain to themselves or to those they love. Even when time has passed, the memory of those moments can remain vivid.

The enemy often uses these memories as weapons. He reminds people of their failures again and again until they begin to believe they are unworthy of love, forgiveness, or a new beginning. Over time, these accusations can distort a person's identity. Instead of seeing themselves as someone capable of growth and transformation, they begin to see themselves only through the lens of their mistakes.

Yet this is not how God sees people. Scripture reminds us: *"There is therefore now no condemnation for those who are in Christ Jesus."* — Romans 8:1

This truth directly challenges the voice of condemnation. Where the enemy accuses, God offers forgiveness. Where shame attempts to imprison the soul, grace opens the door to freedom.

The Woman Surrounded by Accusers

One of the most powerful examples of condemnation in Scripture appears in the story of a woman brought before Jesus by a group of religious leaders. The woman had been caught in adultery. According to the law, the punishment for her sin was severe. The crowd gathered around her with stones in their hands, ready to condemn her publicly.

In that moment, the woman stood surrounded by accusation, shame, and fear. Her past mistake had become the center of everyone's attention. The people around her saw only her sin. They saw only the failure that had brought her to that moment.

But Jesus saw something different. Instead of joining the voices of condemnation, Jesus responded in a way that completely changed the atmosphere.

"Let any one of you who is without sin be the first to throw a stone at her." —John 8:7

One by one, the accusers began to leave. The crowd that had gathered to condemn her slowly disappeared until only Jesus and the woman remained.

Then Jesus spoke words that continue to echo through history: *"Neither do I condemn you. Go now and leave your life of sin."* —John 8:11

These words reveal something profound about the heart of God. Jesus did not ignore the seriousness of sin, but He refused to allow condemnation to have the final word. Grace replaced accusation. Restoration replaced shame.

When the Enemy Attacks Identity

Condemnation does more than remind people of their past mistakes. Its deeper goal is to attack identity. When someone begins to believe the lie that they are permanently broken, they may lose the motivation to pursue healing or growth.

The enemy wants people to believe they are beyond redemption. Yet the message of the gospel declares the opposite. Transformation is always possible. The same God who restored the woman surrounded by accusers continues to restore people today. No mistake is beyond the reach of God's mercy. Condemnation focuses on what a person has done. Grace focuses on who a person can become.

Breaking Free from Self-Hate

For some people, the harshest voice of condemnation does not come from others. It comes from within. Self-hate can quietly grow when people replay painful memories again and again. They may judge themselves more harshly than anyone else ever has. They may believe they deserve punishment instead of healing.

But God's desire for His children is not destruction; it is restoration. The journey toward freedom begins when a person chooses to believe what God says rather than what shame continues to repeat. God's truth has the power to silence accusations that have lingered for years. Healing begins when the voice of grace becomes louder than the voice of condemnation.

A Truth to Remember

Your past may explain some parts of your story, but it does not have the authority to define your future.

The enemy uses condemnation to keep people trapped in yesterday. God uses grace to lead people into tomorrow. The moment a person accepts God's forgiveness, the chains of shame begin to lose their power. Freedom begins where condemnation ends.

Reflection and Prayer

If you have been carrying guilt or shame from your past, take a moment to remember that God's grace is greater than your mistakes. The voice of condemnation may have repeated accusations for years, but that voice does not come from God. God's desire is to restore, not to destroy.

Prayer

Lord, you know every part of my story, including the moments I regret and the mistakes I wish I could change. Help me release the weight of condemnation and receive the forgiveness you freely offer. Teach me to see myself through your grace rather than through my past. Restore my heart, renew my mind, and lead me into the freedom you have prepared for me. Amen.

Chapter 3
When the Heart Feels Heavy: Finding Strength Again

There are seasons in life when the heart feels unusually heavy. A person may move through the day completing responsibilities, speaking with others, and fulfilling expectations, yet inside there is a quiet weight that is difficult to explain. Tasks that once felt simple may require greater effort. Motivation may feel distant for a time, and the mind may feel tired even after rest.

Many people experience moments like this along their journey. Sometimes these seasons arrive after disappointment or unexpected change. At other times they come quietly, without a clear reason. Life continues around them, yet something within feels slower, quieter, and less certain than before. During such moments, it can become easy to question one's strength.

The enemy often takes advantage of these seasons by whispering discouraging thoughts. He may suggest that strength will never return or that the future will always feel as heavy as the present moment. If these thoughts remain unchallenged, they can slowly influence how a person views their life and circumstances. Yet the message of Scripture reminds us that seasons of weariness are not the end of the journey. Many faithful people who walked closely with God also experienced moments when their strength felt limited.

When Strength Feels Distant

Life places many responsibilities upon the human heart. Work, family, expectations, disappointments, and personal challenges can gradually build pressure within the soul. When these pressures accumulate over time, a person may begin to feel as though their inner strength is being stretched further than they expected. During these moments, it is important to remember that feeling weary does not mean a person has lost their purpose. Even people who have experienced great victories sometimes require moments of renewal.

Elijah's Season of Renewal

One powerful example of this appears in the life of the prophet Elijah. Elijah had just witnessed an extraordinary moment when God demonstrated His power before the people of Israel. It was a remarkable victory that revealed God's authority and faithfulness.

Yet shortly afterward, Elijah found himself physically and emotionally exhausted. The journey he had been walking required more strength than he realized. Instead of continuing forward immediately, Elijah entered a quiet place where he rested.

God did not respond with criticism or impatience. Instead, He responded with care. Scripture describes how Elijah rested, and God provided nourishment for him. After Elijah regained strength, God gently spoke to him and guided him forward again. *"The Lord said to him, 'Go back the way you came.'"* — 1 Kings 19:15

This moment reveals something deeply encouraging about the heart of God. When people feel worn down by the journey of life, God often begins the process of restoration by allowing them to rest, regain strength, and rediscover direction.

Elijah's story reminds us that moments of exhaustion do not cancel a person's purpose. Sometimes what feels like a pause in the journey is simply a moment when God is preparing someone for what lies ahead.

When the Soul Needs Renewal

Many people try to push through difficult seasons without giving themselves time to rest. In a world that celebrates constant activity and productivity, it can feel difficult to slow down. Yet renewal often begins when a person allows their heart and mind to pause. Moments of quiet reflection, prayer, and worship help the soul reconnect with the source of true strength. During these moments, perspective begins to change. What once felt overwhelming may begin to feel manageable again. Hope slowly returns, and the mind begins to see possibilities that previously seemed hidden.

A Truth to Remember

One important truth stands at the center of this chapter: Seasons of weariness do not cancel God's purpose for your life. They are often moments when God is quietly restoring strength for the next part of the journey.

Just as Elijah discovered renewed direction after a time of rest, many people find that their greatest clarity comes after allowing their hearts to recover. God continues to guide those who trust Him, even during seasons when the path ahead feels uncertain.

Looking Forward

The heart that feels heavy today may discover renewed strength tomorrow. Life moves through seasons, and God often uses quieter moments to prepare people for greater clarity and purpose ahead. When the soul remembers where true strength comes from, hope begins to grow again. Renewal begins not through pressure or fear, but through trust in God's presence and guidance.

Reflection and Prayer

If you are walking through a season where your heart feels tired or burdened, remember that God understands every step of your journey. He sees your efforts, your struggles, and your desire to keep moving forward. Just as He restored Elijah, He is able to restore strength and clarity in your life. Take a moment to rest in that promise.

Prayer

Lord, you know every season of my life. When my strength feels limited, remind me that your strength never fails. Help me find rest in your presence and trust your guidance for the path ahead. Renew my courage, restore my hope, and lead me forward with confidence in your care. Amen.

Chapter 4
The Pain of Rejection and Feeling Invisible

Rejection may wound the heart, but it cannot cancel the purpose God has placed within a life.

There are moments when a person begins to feel unnoticed. They may be surrounded by people, working hard and doing their best to contribute, yet something inside whispers that their presence does not matter. Efforts seem overlooked. Words go unheard. The recognition they hoped for never seems to arrive.

Over time, experiences like this can leave a quiet mark on the heart. Many people know what it feels like to be misunderstood or overlooked. Sometimes rejection comes from strangers. At other times it comes from people whose acceptance mattered deeply—friends, family members, colleagues, or others whose opinions carried great weight.

When rejection occurs repeatedly, it can slowly shape how a person sees themselves. Some begin to believe they are simply not valued. Others withdraw, protecting themselves from future disappointment.

The enemy often uses these moments to plant subtle lies in the heart. He whispers that a person is not important. He suggests that their efforts do not matter or that their presence makes little difference. Yet rejection does not always reveal a person's worth. Often, it simply reveals the limitations of the people who failed to recognize it.

When Rejection Comes From Those Closest to Us

Rejection can be especially painful when it comes from people who were expected to offer support. When encouragement is absent from those closest to us, the experience can create deep confusion. Questions begin to form within the heart.

Why was I treated this way? Why was I not accepted? Did I do something wrong? These questions can linger for years if they are not answered with truth. Yet many people in Scripture experienced similar moments. One of the clearest examples is found in the life of Joseph.

Joseph's Story of Rejection

Joseph was the son of Jacob and was loved deeply by his father. Yet his relationship with his brothers became strained as jealousy began to grow in their hearts. Instead of celebrating Joseph's life and calling, his brothers began to resent him. Their jealousy eventually turned into rejection. One day they decided to remove Joseph from their lives completely.

Joseph was taken far away from his family and sold as a servant in a foreign land. In a single moment, the life he knew disappeared. The people who should have protected him had become the ones who pushed him away.

From a human perspective, Joseph's future seemed uncertain. Yet God had not abandoned Joseph's story. Even in a place far from home, God continued working quietly in Joseph's life. The path Joseph walked was not easy, but step by step God guided him through each season.

Years later Joseph found himself in a position of great responsibility and influence in Egypt. Looking back at his journey, Joseph recognized something powerful about the rejection he had experienced. *"You intended to harm me, but God intended it for good."* — Genesis 50:20

Joseph understood that the rejection he experienced had not destroyed his purpose. God had used it to position him for something greater.

When Rejection Tries to Redefine Identity

One of the enemy's strategies is to use rejection to reshape how a person sees themselves. When someone experiences repeated rejection, they may begin to believe that something is wrong with them. They may question their abilities, their worth, or their place in the world. Yet rejection does not determine identity. Human opinions often change, but God's perspective remains steady.

Throughout Scripture we see that many individuals who were overlooked or misunderstood by others were later used by God in remarkable ways. David was overlooked when the prophet Samuel came searching for Israel's next king. Ruth entered a new land as a widow with an uncertain future. Moses once believed he was not capable of speaking before leaders. Yet God saw potential where others saw limitation. The opinions of people did not determine the outcome of their lives.

A Truth to Remember

There is a truth that every person who has experienced rejection must eventually learn: Rejection does not cancel purpose; sometimes it redirects it.

Joseph's story reminds us that God often continues working behind the scenes, even when circumstances seem unfair or confusing. What appears to be a closed door may simply be the beginning of a different path. God's plans are not limited by the opinions or decisions of other people.

Looking Beyond the Moment

When rejection occurs, it can feel deeply personal. Yet with time and reflection, many people discover that those moments were not the end of their story. Sometimes rejection moves people away from places where they were not meant to remain. Sometimes it creates opportunities that would never have appeared otherwise.

Joseph's journey shows that God can transform even painful experiences into moments of preparation. The same God who guided Joseph continues to guide people today. No moment of rejection has the authority to erase the purpose God has written into a life.

Reflection and Prayer

If you have experienced rejection or moments when you felt invisible, remember that your worth is not determined by the approval of others. God sees the value within your life even when others fail to recognize it. Just as He guided Joseph through seasons of uncertainty, He continues to guide every life that trusts Him.

Prayer

Lord, when rejection makes my heart feel uncertain, remind me that my worth comes from you. Help me see my life through your eyes rather than through the opinions of others. Guide my steps, strengthen my confidence, and help me trust the purpose you have placed within my life. Amen.

Chapter 5
The Trap of Comparison

Comparison quietly steals joy by convincing the heart that someone else's journey is more valuable than your own.

There are moments when people begin measuring their lives against the lives of others. It may happen quietly while listening to someone share their achievements, observing the progress of a colleague, or noticing the recognition someone else receives. What begins as simple observation can slowly turn into comparison.

At first, the thoughts may seem harmless. A person notices another individual moving forward in life and begins to wonder why their own progress feels slower. They see opportunities opening for others and begin to question whether their own efforts are being overlooked. Gradually, comparison begins to shape how a person views their own story. Instead of recognizing the value of their own journey, they begin evaluating themselves according to someone else's path. Achievements that once felt meaningful begin to seem smaller. Gratitude slowly fades as attention shifts toward what others appear to have.

The enemy often uses comparison in subtle ways. Rather than attacking a person directly, he encourages them to constantly look at someone else's life. When attention is focused outward, people begin to lose sight of the purpose and growth unfolding within their own lives.

When Someone Else's Success Feels Personal

Comparison often becomes strongest when people feel their efforts are not being noticed. They may have worked diligently, invested their time and energy, and remained faithful to their responsibilities. Yet when someone else receives recognition or advancement, it can create a quiet sense of frustration.

Questions begin to form within the mind: Why is their life moving faster than mine? Why did that opportunity go to them instead of me? Am I falling behind?

These thoughts may appear small at first, but when they repeat over time, they begin to influence the heart. Joy becomes difficult to maintain when comparison becomes the lens through which life is viewed.

Saul's Struggle With Comparison

The Bible provides a powerful example of how comparison can influence the heart through the story of King Saul. Saul had been chosen as the first king of Israel. At the beginning of his leadership, he carried great responsibility and had been entrusted with guiding the nation. Yet as time passed, another young man named David began gaining recognition for his courage and faith.

After David defeated Goliath, the people celebrated his victory. *"Saul has slain his thousands, and David his tens of thousands."* — 1 Samuel 18:7

When Saul heard these words, something changed within him. Instead of celebrating David's courage and faith, Saul began to feel threatened by it. The attention David received stirred insecurity within Saul's heart. From that moment forward, Saul began viewing David not as a fellow servant of God, but as a rival. What began as comparison slowly developed into jealousy.

Saul allowed that comparison to influence his decisions and shape his actions. His focus shifted away from the responsibilities God had given him and toward competing with someone else. In the end, comparison robbed Saul of peace and clarity.

The Danger of Looking Sideways

When a person constantly looks sideways at the lives of others, they often lose sight of the path directly in front of them.

God's guidance for each life is unique. If David had focused on comparing himself with Saul, he might never have developed the courage and faith that later defined his leadership. His journey required patience and preparation during seasons when recognition was not immediate.

Comparison can distract people from the work God is doing in their own lives. Instead of developing their gifts, they begin watching the progress of others. Instead of strengthening their own purpose, they begin evaluating themselves according to someone else's story. Purpose grows best when attention remains focused on the direction God has given.

Learning to Celebrate Others

One of the healthiest responses to comparison is learning to celebrate the success of others. When people learn to genuinely rejoice with others, comparison loses its power to discourage the heart. Another person's achievement does not reduce the possibilities available to you. God's plans for each life remain unique and purposeful.

Learning to celebrate others creates freedom within the heart. It replaces insecurity with gratitude and replaces rivalry with encouragement.

Truths to Remember

Two important reminders can protect the heart from comparison: Your journey is not behind someone else's—it is simply different. And equally important: God's purpose for your life cannot be measured by someone else's progress.

The progress of another person does not determine your position. God continues to guide each life according to His wisdom and timing.

Pause and Reflect

Take a moment to reflect on the questions below:

• Have I been comparing my life with someone else's journey?

• In what ways has comparison affected my joy or confidence?

• What blessings or opportunities might I be overlooking in my own life?
• How can I begin focusing more on the path God has given me rather than the path of others?

Reflection allows the heart to return to truth.

Prayer
Lord, help me release the habit of comparing my life with others. Teach me to appreciate the journey you have designed for me. Give me the ability to celebrate the success of others while remaining confident in the purpose you have placed within my own life. Fill my heart with gratitude and guide my steps according to your plan. Amen.

Chapter 6
Recognizing the Blessings You Already Have

Sometimes the greatest blessings in life become invisible when the heart focuses only on what is missing.

There are seasons when people become so focused on what they do not have that they begin to overlook what is already present in their lives. This often happens gradually. A person notices what others possess—opportunities, recognition, resources, or achievements—and quietly begins comparing those things to their own circumstances. Over time, the mind begins concentrating on what appears absent rather than on what is already present. What once felt like a blessing may begin to feel ordinary.

Gratitude slowly fades—not because blessings disappeared, but because attention shifted toward what seems missing. The enemy often uses this subtle shift in focus to create dissatisfaction within the heart. When people become preoccupied with what they lack, they begin to overlook the many ways God has already provided for them.

When Dissatisfaction Quietly Grows

Dissatisfaction rarely begins with major events. Most often it develops through small thoughts that repeat themselves. A person may begin thinking:
"If only I had what they have." "If my life looked like theirs, things would be better." "If I had more opportunities, more support, or more recognition, I would finally feel fulfilled." These thoughts slowly influence perspective.

Instead of seeing life through gratitude, the heart begins interpreting everything through absence. Even genuine blessings can begin to feel insufficient when the mind becomes trained to notice only what is lacking.

When Blessings Become Familiar

Another reason people sometimes overlook what they already have is familiarity. When something becomes part of everyday life, it can slowly lose the sense of wonder it once carried. A person may once have prayed for an opportunity, a relationship, a job, or a new beginning. At the time, it felt like an answer to prayer. Gratitude filled the heart because the blessing was new.

But as time passes and life becomes routine, what once felt extraordinary can begin to feel ordinary. The mind gradually stops noticing it. The same blessing that once inspired gratitude may begin to feel expected rather than appreciated.

This shift happens quietly. Without realizing it, people sometimes begin searching for something new while overlooking what has already been given to them. Yet many blessings reveal their true value only when they are recognized with gratitude.

The Story of the Israelites in the Wilderness

Scripture gives a powerful example of this pattern through the journey of the Israelites in the wilderness. After God delivered them from slavery in Egypt, they began traveling toward the land that had been promised to them. Along the way, God continued providing for them in remarkable ways.

Food appeared daily through manna. Water was provided in difficult places. Guidance came through God's presence as they moved forward. Yet despite these provisions, many among the people began focusing on what they believed they had lost. They remembered the food they once had in Egypt and began longing for it again. Instead of recognizing the freedom they had received and the daily provision they were experiencing, their attention turned toward what seemed missing. Their perspective shifted from gratitude to complaint. In those moments, they could not clearly see what God was already doing around them. The blessings present in their lives became difficult to recognize because their focus had moved elsewhere.

When Perspective Changes Everything

The difference between gratitude and dissatisfaction often lies in perspective. Two people can experience the same circumstances, yet view them completely differently. One person may recognize opportunities, growth, and provision. Another may see only limitations and obstacles.

When perspective becomes centered on what is missing, joy becomes difficult to sustain. But when the heart learns to recognize what is already present, gratitude begins to grow again.

Gratitude does not ignore challenges. Rather, it allows people to see that even in imperfect situations, God continues providing guidance, strength, and support.

Gratitude Restores Clarity

Gratitude has the power to restore clarity to the heart. When a person intentionally begins recognizing the good that already exists in their life, something begins to shift inside them. The mind becomes less focused on what is missing and more aware of what has already been provided. Small moments begin to matter again. A supportive conversation, an opportunity to grow, a new lesson learned, or even the simple ability to continue moving forward becomes meaningful.

Gratitude does not mean life is perfect. Rather, it means recognizing that even in imperfect circumstances, there are still signs of God's faithfulness present along the journey.

When gratitude grows, dissatisfaction begins to lose its influence. The heart becomes lighter, and hope begins to return.

Truth to Remember

Gratitude helps the heart recognize blessings that comparison often hides. When attention returns to the gifts already present—relationships, opportunities, growth, and daily provisions—the heart begins to rediscover peace.

The Israelites eventually learned that God's faithfulness was not limited to a single moment of deliverance. It continued to appear each day along their journey.

The same truth applies today. God's provision often appears in ways that become visible only when the heart begins to look for them.

Guided Reflection

Take a quiet moment to consider your own life. Are there areas where your attention has been drawn more toward what seems absent rather than toward what is already present?

Sometimes people become so focused on future hopes or unmet expectations that they overlook the ways God has already been faithful. When perspective shifts toward gratitude, many blessings that once seemed ordinary begin to shine with new meaning. Learning to notice those blessings can transform how the heart experiences daily life.

Pause and Reflect

• Have I been focusing more on what I lack than on what I already have?

• What blessings in my life might I have overlooked recently?
• How might gratitude change the way I see my current situation?
• What is one thing I can thank God for today?

Prayer

Lord, help me recognize the blessings you have already placed in my life. When my thoughts begin focusing on what is missing, guide my heart back to gratitude. Teach me to see your faithfulness in both the small and great moments of life. Fill my heart with thankfulness and help me walk forward with trust in your provision. Amen.

Chapter 7
The Power of Words and Confessions

Words are not merely sounds spoken into the air; they often shape the way the heart sees the future.

Every day people speak hundreds of words—about their lives, their circumstances, their hopes, and their struggles. Most of these words feel ordinary. They are spoken quickly during conversations, moments of frustration, or quiet reflections about the day. Yet over time, the words people speak can begin to influence how they see themselves and the direction they believe their lives are taking.

A person who repeatedly speaks discouraging words about their future may begin to believe those words deeply. In the same way, words filled with hope and faith can gradually strengthen the heart.

The enemy understands this well. One of his subtle strategies is to influence the way people speak about their lives. When negative words become a habit, they slowly shape the thoughts of the mind and the expectations of the heart.

Without realizing it, a person may begin declaring limitations over their own life.

"I will never succeed." "Nothing good ever works out for me." "My situation will never change."

Although these words may be spoken casually, they can slowly reinforce discouragement within the mind. Over time, the heart begins to believe the story those words are telling.

How Words Shape Perspective

Words often reveal what the mind has been focusing on. When a person consistently speaks about difficulties, disappointments, and fears, those concerns begin to dominate their perspective. The mind becomes trained to notice problems more easily than possibilities.

But when words begin reflecting hope, gratitude, and faith, the heart gradually begins seeing life differently. Words help shape perspective.

This does not mean that challenges should be ignored or denied. Life includes real difficulties that must be acknowledged with honesty.

However, the way people speak about those challenges can influence whether they feel overwhelmed by them or strengthened to face them.

When Words Become Habits

Many people do not realize how easily words become habits. A person may begin by expressing frustration about a temporary difficulty. At first, the words simply describe the situation. But when the same words are repeated again and again, they begin to form a pattern. Over time, those words become familiar. The mind begins accepting them as normal descriptions of reality.

Someone who repeatedly says, *"Nothing ever works out for me,"* may eventually begin expecting disappointment before opportunities even appear. In the same way, a person who regularly expresses gratitude or hope begins training their mind to look for positive possibilities. Words spoken frequently begin shaping the expectations of the heart.

A Biblical Example: David's Words of Confidence

One powerful example of the influence of words can be seen in the story of David when he faced Goliath.

The giant Goliath stood before the army of Israel, speaking words intended to intimidate and discourage them. Many soldiers felt fear because of the way the situation appeared. Yet David responded differently.

Instead of repeating words of fear, David spoke with confidence about God's presence and faithfulness. David declared that the battle did not depend on human strength alone, but on the power of God. His words reflected trust rather than defeat. *"The battle is the Lord's."* — 1 Samuel 17:47

Those words did more than express David's belief. They strengthened his courage and reminded others that the situation was not beyond God's ability to handle. David's confidence grew because his words aligned with his faith.

When Words Begin to Change Direction

Many people underestimate the influence of their everyday speech. Small statements repeated over time can quietly shape the expectations a person holds about their future. When discouraging words are repeated long enough, they begin to sound like permanent truths. But when hopeful and faith-filled words are spoken consistently, they gradually reshape the atmosphere of the mind.

Words have the ability to strengthen courage. They can also renew hope when circumstances feel uncertain. Choosing words carefully is not about pretending life is perfect. Rather, it is about allowing truth and faith to guide the language of the heart.

The Power of Encouraging Words

Words also carry the ability to strengthen others. A single encouraging sentence can sometimes change how a person views themselves or their circumstances. Many people remember moments when someone spoke words that lifted their spirit during a difficult time.

Encouragement has a way of restoring hope. Just as negative words can discourage the heart, positive and faith-filled words can remind people of their strength, their potential, and the possibilities ahead of them. When people choose words that bring encouragement, they help create an atmosphere where hope and courage can grow. In this way, words do more than describe life—they help shape the emotional and spiritual environment around us.

Truth to Remember

There is an important reminder that can transform how people speak about their lives: The words you speak repeatedly often shape the direction you begin to believe is possible. When words align with faith, hope, and gratitude, they create space for confidence and perseverance to grow. Over time, those words strengthen the heart to continue moving forward.

Guided Reflection

Take a moment to think about the words you often use when speaking about your life. Do your words reflect hope and trust, or do they often focus on discouragement and limitation?

Everyone experiences moments when frustration or disappointment influences their speech. Yet awareness creates an opportunity to change direction. When people begin choosing words that reflect faith and gratitude, their perspective slowly begins to shift. The heart becomes stronger and more hopeful.

Pause and Reflect

• What kinds of words do I often use when speaking about my life or future?

• Are my words strengthening hope or reinforcing discouragement?

• How might my outlook change if I began speaking more words of faith and gratitude?
• What is one encouraging truth I can begin speaking over my life today?

Prayer

Lord, help me become more aware of the words I speak each day. Guide my thoughts and my speech so that they reflect faith, hope, and trust in you. When I feel discouraged, remind me to speak words that strengthen my heart rather than weaken it. May my words reflect the confidence that comes from knowing you are guiding my life. Amen.

Chapter 8
Guarding the Mind

The battle for the soul often begins quietly in the mind. Many people assume that the greatest battles in life take place in visible circumstances—difficult situations, relationships, or unexpected challenges. Yet long before those struggles appear outwardly, something is often happening within the mind.

Thoughts shape how people interpret the events around them. They influence emotions, decisions, and expectations about the future. When certain thoughts repeat often enough, they begin forming beliefs about what is possible and what is not. For this reason, guarding the mind becomes an essential part of protecting the heart.

The enemy understands that if he can influence a person's thoughts, he can gradually influence how that person sees themselves, their circumstances, and even their future. Many struggles begin not in outward events, but in quiet thoughts that slowly grow stronger over time.

How Thoughts Influence the Heart

Every day the mind processes countless thoughts. Some of those thoughts bring encouragement, creativity, and hope. Others may introduce doubt, worry, or discouragement.

When discouraging thoughts repeat frequently, they can begin shaping how a person views life. Someone who repeatedly thinks, *"Nothing ever works out for me,"* may gradually begin expecting disappointment before opportunities even appear.

In the same way, a person who trains their mind to notice possibilities, gratitude, and faith begins developing a different outlook. The thoughts that receive the most attention often become the thoughts that shape the heart.

A Real-Life Scenario

Consider a person who experiences disappointment at work. Perhaps an opportunity they hoped for was given to someone else. At first, the situation may simply feel discouraging. But then certain thoughts begin repeating themselves: "Maybe I am not good enough." "People probably don't value my work." "I will never move forward."

If those thoughts remain unchallenged, they may slowly become accepted as truth. Yet the situation itself may not have meant those things at all.

This example shows how the mind can sometimes create conclusions that influence emotions and confidence. Learning to recognize these patterns is an important step toward guarding the mind.

Scripture and the Discipline of Thought

The Bible speaks clearly about the importance of directing our thoughts wisely. Scripture encourages believers to focus on thoughts that bring truth and encouragement.

"Finally, brothers and sisters, whatever is true, whatever is noble, whatever is right, whatever is pure, whatever is lovely, whatever is admirable—if anything is excellent or praiseworthy—think about such things." — Philippians 4:8

This verse reminds us that the mind does not have to wander without guidance. People can learn to direct their attention toward thoughts that strengthen their perspective rather than weaken it.

This does not mean ignoring difficulties. Instead, it means choosing to focus on truth, hope, and what is constructive rather than allowing discouragement to dominate the mind.

Learning to Guard the Mind

Guarding the mind begins with awareness. When people become aware of the thoughts influencing their emotions, they gain the ability to evaluate those thoughts more carefully.

Some thoughts bring clarity and encouragement. Others may introduce fear, discouragement, or unnecessary worry. When a discouraging thought appears, it can be helpful to pause and ask: Is this thought helpful? Is it true? Is it guiding me toward hope or toward discouragement?

This simple awareness allows people to gently redirect their attention toward thoughts that strengthen their inner life. Over time, this practice creates a healthier mental environment where peace and confidence can grow.

Truth to Remember

The thoughts that receive the most attention gradually shape the direction of the heart. When people learn to guard their minds carefully, they create space for peace, clarity, and faith to grow. The mind becomes a place where hope is cultivated rather than where discouragement takes root.

Guided Reflection

Take a moment to consider the thoughts that most often occupy your mind. Do they bring encouragement and clarity, or do they frequently introduce doubt and worry?

Everyone experiences difficult thoughts at times. Yet learning to recognize them allows the heart to choose a healthier direction. By intentionally focusing on thoughts that reflect truth and hope, the mind can become a place of strength rather than struggle.

Pause and Reflect

- What thoughts do I find repeating most often in my mind?
- Do those thoughts strengthen my confidence or weaken it?
- How might my outlook change if I focused more on thoughts that bring hope and truth?
- What is one encouraging thought I can intentionally hold onto today?

Prayer

Lord, help me become aware of the thoughts that influence my heart. Guide my mind toward what is true, hopeful, and life-giving. When discouraging thoughts appear, give me the wisdom to replace them with truth and faith. May my mind become a place where your peace and guidance are present each day. Amen.

Chapter 9
The Danger of Isolation

The battles of the soul often feel heavier when they are carried alone. There are moments in life when people quietly withdraw from others. Sometimes the withdrawal is intentional. A person may feel misunderstood or discouraged and decide that being alone feels easier than explaining their feelings. At other times isolation happens gradually. Busy schedules, disappointments, or personal struggles slowly create distance between a person and the supportive relationships around them.

At first, solitude can seem harmless. In fact, there are moments when quiet reflection is healthy and necessary. Time alone can help people think clearly, pray, and regain perspective. But when isolation becomes a habit rather than a temporary moment of reflection, it can slowly weaken the heart.

Human beings were not designed to face every challenge alone. Encouragement, support, and shared understanding from others often strengthen people during seasons when life feels overwhelming. When those connections disappear, even small struggles can begin to feel heavier.

The enemy often uses isolation as a strategy because a person who feels alone may begin believing that no one understands their struggles. When that belief grows strong, the heart can begin losing hope.

When Isolation Feels Safer

Many people withdraw from others not because they dislike people, but because they want to protect themselves from further disappointment. Perhaps they trusted someone who later betrayed their confidence. Maybe they reached out for support and felt misunderstood. Experiences like these can make a person hesitant to open their heart again. Over time, they may begin telling themselves that it is safer to keep their struggles private.

"I will handle this on my own." "I don't want to bother anyone with my problems." "No one would really understand anyway."

These thoughts may feel reasonable at first. Yet when they repeat often enough, they slowly build a wall between a person and the encouragement they might otherwise receive. Isolation does not always begin with loneliness. Sometimes it begins with the belief that facing challenges alone is the only option.

A Real-Life Scenario

Imagine someone going through a difficult season in life. Perhaps they have experienced disappointment in their career or tension in their relationships. At first, they mention their struggles to a few friends, but the responses they receive feel dismissive or rushed. Instead of trying again, they decide to keep their thoughts to themselves.

Days turn into weeks, and weeks turn into months. Gradually they stop sharing their concerns with anyone. Although people around them may not notice immediately, the weight they carry inside grows heavier over time. What might have felt manageable with encouragement begins to feel overwhelming when faced alone.

This example reflects a pattern many people experience. When isolation becomes a habit, the mind begins carrying burdens that were never meant to be carried without support.

Elijah's Moment of Exhaustion

Scripture provides a powerful example of this experience in the life of the prophet Elijah. Elijah had just experienced an extraordinary victory when God demonstrated His power before the people of Israel.

Yet shortly afterward Elijah found himself exhausted and discouraged. He traveled into the wilderness and sat alone under a tree. In that moment Elijah believed he was completely alone in his struggle.

But God did not leave him in isolation. Instead, God responded with care and restoration. Elijah was given rest, nourishment, and renewed direction. Later he also discovered that there were others who still remained faithful. Elijah's story reminds us that moments of exhaustion and discouragement are part of the human journey.

Yet even during those moments, God provides support and guidance in ways we may not immediately recognize.

Moses and Aaron: The Strength of Support

Another powerful example of shared strength appears in the story of Moses. When God called Moses to lead the people of Israel, Moses initially felt overwhelmed by the responsibility. He doubted his ability to speak and lead such a large nation.

But God did not expect Moses to carry that responsibility alone. Instead, God provided Aaron to stand beside him and support him. Scripture records

God saying: *"Is not Aaron the Levite your brother? I know that he can speak well… He will speak to the people for you."* — Exodus 4:14–16

Aaron became a voice of support and partnership in Moses' journey. Later, during a battle with the Amalekites, Moses stood on a hill while Joshua led the army below. As Moses raised his hands, the people of Israel began to prevail. But as the battle continued, Moses became tired. Aaron and Hur came alongside him and held up his hands so that he could continue until victory was secured.

"When Moses' hands grew tired, they took a stone and put it under him and he sat on it. Aaron and Hur held his hands up—one on one side, one on the other—so that his hands remained steady till sunset." — Exodus 17:12

This moment reveals a powerful truth. Even great leaders sometimes need others to support them during difficult moments. Victory was not achieved by Moses standing alone, but through shared strength.

The Strength of Shared Encouragement

One of the greatest sources of strength during difficult seasons is encouragement from others.

Sometimes a simple conversation can bring clarity to a situation that once felt overwhelming. Hearing someone say, *"You are not alone,"* can restore hope to a weary heart. Encouragement reminds people that their struggles are not unique.

Others have faced similar moments and have continued moving forward. Community also provides perspective. When someone feels discouraged, their view of the situation may become narrow. But when trusted friends or mentors speak into the situation, they often help reveal possibilities that the discouraged person could not see alone.

Scripture reminds us of the strength found in companionship: *"Two are better than one… If either of them falls down, one can help the other up."* — Ecclesiastes 4:9–10

This is why relationships built on trust and encouragement are so valuable. They strengthen people when their own strength feels limited.

Truth to Remember

There is an important truth that many people rediscover during difficult seasons: Isolation magnifies burdens, but shared encouragement restores strength. The presence of supportive relationships can lighten emotional weight and renew hope. Even when circumstances remain challenging, knowing that others care and understand can make the journey feel less overwhelming.

Guided Reflection

Consider your own experiences during difficult seasons. Have there been moments when you felt tempted to withdraw from others rather than share what you were going through?

Many people discover that isolation initially feels easier but eventually makes the struggle feel heavier. Allowing trusted individuals to walk alongside you can bring strength, wisdom, and encouragement during times when you need it most.

Pause and Reflect

• Have there been times when I chose isolation instead of seeking support?
• What fears or experiences may have influenced that decision?
• Who in my life could provide encouragement or wisdom during difficult seasons?
• What small step could I take toward reconnecting with supportive relationships?

Prayer

Lord, help me remember that I do not have to face every challenge alone. Guide me toward relationships that bring encouragement, wisdom, and support. When I feel tempted to withdraw from others, remind me that community can strengthen my heart. Help me both receive and offer encouragement to those around me. Amen.

PART II

Practices That Restore the Soul

Learning the spiritual practices that renew strength and restore hope.

Chapter 10

The Power of Prayer

Prayer is not merely a religious routine; it is a conversation that reconnects the human heart with the source of strength and guidance.

Throughout history, people have turned to prayer during moments of uncertainty, gratitude, and need. In its simplest form, prayer is the act of bringing one's thoughts, hopes, concerns, and thanksgiving before God.

For many people, prayer begins as a quiet moment of reflection. It may occur during the early hours of the morning, in the stillness of the evening, or during a brief pause in the middle of a busy day. Yet prayer becomes far more powerful when it moves beyond routine and becomes a sincere conversation with God.

Prayer is not reserved only for perfect moments. Often it becomes most meaningful during seasons when life feels uncertain, when questions seem unanswered, or when the heart simply needs peace. In these moments, the heart finds a place to release worries, express gratitude, and seek wisdom for the path ahead.

When Life Feels Beyond Our Strength

There are seasons when challenges feel larger than our ability to manage them. A person may face difficult decisions, unexpected changes, or situations that seem to have no clear solution. During these times it can feel as though every effort made to solve the problem brings little progress.

In such moments, prayer offers something unique. Instead of carrying every burden alone, a person places those concerns into God's hands. Prayer shifts the focus from human limitations to divine guidance. This shift does not mean that difficulties disappear immediately. Rather, it reminds the heart that we are not navigating life without help.

Prayer opens a door for peace and wisdom to enter situations that once felt overwhelming. Scripture offers this encouragement: *"Cast all your anxiety on him because he cares for you."* — 1 Peter 5:7

This promise reminds us that God invites us to bring every concern before Him.

A Real-Life Scenario

Consider someone facing a major decision in their life. Perhaps they are considering a career change, dealing with financial uncertainty, or trying to resolve tension in a relationship. The situation may feel confusing because every option carries its own risks and uncertainties. They may spend hours thinking about the problem, discussing it with others, or searching for solutions. Yet clarity still feels distant.

Then they pause and bring the situation before God in prayer. In that moment something begins to shift. The problem may not vanish immediately, but the heart becomes calmer. Anxiety begins to loosen its grip, and a new perspective slowly emerges. This illustrates one of the quiet strengths of prayer—it helps the heart move from worry toward trust.

Scripture encourages this approach: *"Do not be anxious about anything, but in every situation, by prayer and petition, with thanksgiving, present your requests to God."*
— Philippians 4:6

This verse reminds us that prayer allows every concern to be placed before God.

The Example of Jesus in Prayer

One of the most powerful examples of prayer appears in the life of Jesus. Throughout His ministry, Jesus frequently withdrew from crowds in order to spend time in prayer. Even during moments when people were seeking His attention, He made space to reconnect with God.

Scripture records one such moment: *"Very early in the morning, while it was still dark, Jesus got up, left the house and went off to a solitary place, where he prayed."* — Mark 1:35

This verse reveals an important truth. Even Jesus, who carried great responsibility and influence, understood the importance of stepping away from the noise of life to reconnect with God through prayer. Prayer was not an afterthought in His life; it was a source of strength and guidance.

Prayer Brings Clarity

One of the quiet gifts of prayer is clarity. When people pray sincerely, they create space for reflection and spiritual awareness. Thoughts that once felt tangled begin to settle.

Sometimes prayer does not provide immediate answers, but it often provides something equally valuable—peace. That peace allows people to think more clearly and approach their circumstances with patience and wisdom. Instead of reacting quickly out of fear or frustration, prayer encourages thoughtful decisions guided by trust.

Scripture reminds us of this peace: *"And the peace of God, which surpasses all understanding, will guard your hearts and your minds in Christ Jesus."* — Philippians 4:7

When prayer becomes a habit, peace often follows.

Prayer Strengthens the Heart

Prayer also strengthens the heart during difficult seasons. When someone speaks honestly to God about their fears, disappointments, and hopes, they release emotional weight that may have been carried silently. The act of expressing those concerns can bring relief and renewal.

Prayer reminds people that their struggles are seen and understood by God. Even when solutions are not immediate, the knowledge that God listens brings comfort and reassurance.

Truth to Remember

Prayer connects human weakness with divine strength. It reminds us that we do not face life's challenges relying only on our own understanding. When people approach God sincerely, they often discover that peace and guidance appear in ways they did not expect.

Prayer does not remove every challenge, but it strengthens the heart to walk through those challenges with courage and trust.

Guided Reflection

Take a moment to reflect on your own experience with prayer. Do you view prayer as a routine activity, or as an opportunity to have an honest conversation with God?

Many people discover that prayer becomes more meaningful when it includes both speaking and listening—expressing concerns while also allowing quiet moments for reflection and trust. When prayer becomes part of daily life, it often transforms how the heart responds to challenges.

Pause and Reflect

- How often do I bring my concerns before God in prayer?
- Do I see prayer as a routine, or as a sincere conversation with God?
- What situation in my life right now could benefit from prayer and reflection?
- How might my outlook change if I approached challenges with prayer first?

Prayer

Lord, thank you for inviting me to speak with you through prayer. Help me remember that I can bring every concern, decision, and hope before you. Teach me to trust your wisdom when life feels uncertain. Fill my heart with peace and guide my steps as I continue forward. Amen.

Chapter 11
The Strength Found in Worship

Worship has the power to lift the heart above circumstances and remind the soul of God's presence. There are seasons in life when burdens feel heavy and answers seem distant. During those moments people often search for something that can restore their sense of hope and strength.

One of the most powerful ways the human heart reconnects with God during difficult seasons is through worship.

Worship is more than music or singing. At its core, worship is the act of honoring God with gratitude, reverence, and trust. It is the expression of the heart that acknowledges God's presence, goodness, and authority even when life feels uncertain. When people worship, they shift their attention away from the weight of their circumstances and toward the greatness of God. This shift in focus can change the atmosphere within the heart.

Worship reminds the soul that no situation is beyond God's ability to guide and restore. Scripture reminds us of the importance of worship: *"God is spirit, and his*

worshipers must worship in the Spirit and in truth."
—John 4:24

Worship reconnects the human heart with the living presence of God.

When Circumstances Feel Overwhelming

Life sometimes presents situations that appear larger than our ability to solve them. Unexpected challenges, emotional burdens, and uncertain futures can cause people to feel discouraged. In those moments it becomes easy to focus entirely on the difficulty itself.

But worship introduces a different perspective. Instead of concentrating only on the problem, worship redirects the heart toward the One who is greater than the problem. When people worship, they begin remembering God's faithfulness in the past. That remembrance often renews confidence that God continues to work even when solutions are not immediately visible.

Worship helps the heart move from anxiety toward trust. Scripture expresses this truth beautifully: *"The Lord is my strength and my shield; my heart trusts in him, and he helps me. My heart leaps for joy, and with my song I praise him."* — Psalm 28:7

When worship rises from the heart, strength often follows.

A Real-Life Scenario

Imagine someone who has been carrying a heavy emotional burden for weeks. Perhaps they are dealing with uncertainty about their future or facing challenges in their relationships. Their mind feels tired from constantly trying to find answers.

One evening they decide to spend a few quiet moments listening to worship music or reflecting on God's goodness. At first nothing dramatic seems to happen. But slowly something begins to change.

Their breathing becomes calmer. The tension in their thoughts begins to soften. Instead of focusing entirely on the problem, their attention shifts toward God's presence and faithfulness. The circumstances may remain the same, but the heart begins to feel strengthened.

This is one of the quiet gifts of worship—it renews the inner life.

Worship in Difficult Moments
The Story of Paul and Silas

One remarkable example of the power of worship appears in the story of Paul and Silas. After faithfully preaching the message of Christ, Paul and Silas were arrested, beaten, and thrown into prison. Their feet were placed in chains, and they were confined in a dark cell.

From a human perspective, this situation could have easily produced fear, anger, or despair. Yet their response was completely different. Instead of allowing discouragement to control their hearts, they began praying and worshiping God. Scripture records this powerful moment: *"About midnight Paul and Silas were praying and singing hymns to God, and the other prisoners were listening to them."* — Acts 16:25

Imagine the scene. Two men sitting in a dark prison, surrounded by chains and uncertainty, yet choosing to lift their voices in worship. Their circumstances had not changed. The prison doors were still closed. Their chains were still in place. But their hearts were focused on God rather than their suffering. Then something remarkable happened.

"Suddenly there was such a violent earthquake that the foundations of the prison were shaken. At once all the prison doors flew open, and everyone's chains came loose." — Acts 16:26

Worship filled the prison, and the atmosphere changed. The story of Paul and Silas reveals an important truth: Worship has the power to shift spiritual atmospheres. Even when circumstances seem immovable, worship reminds the heart that God remains present and powerful.

How Worship Changes the Atmosphere of the Heart

Worship often transforms the inner atmosphere of a person's life. When people focus only on their challenges, their minds can become overwhelmed with worry or discouragement. But when worship fills the heart, those same thoughts begin losing their influence.

Worship reminds the soul of God's character. It reminds people that God remains faithful, powerful, and present even when circumstances appear uncertain. This renewed awareness strengthens courage and restores peace. Scripture reminds us:

"Enter his gates with thanksgiving and his courts with praise; give thanks to him and praise his name." — Psalm 100:4

Praise and worship open the heart to God's presence.

Worship as a Daily Practice

Worship does not need to be limited to special gatherings or formal settings. Many people discover that worship becomes most meaningful when it becomes part of everyday life.

It may happen through music, prayer, gratitude, or quiet reflection on God's goodness. Some people worship while walking, driving, or beginning their day with a moment of gratitude. These simple moments of worship remind the heart that God's presence is not distant. He remains close to those who seek Him. Over time, worship becomes more than an occasional activity—it becomes a lifestyle.

Truth to Remember

Worship lifts the heart above circumstances and reconnects the soul with God's presence. When people worship sincerely, they rediscover strength that does not depend on the stability of their circumstances.

Their confidence begins resting in God's faithfulness rather than in temporary situations.

Guided Reflection

Take a moment to consider how worship appears in your life. Do you reserve worship only for certain moments, or do you allow it to become part of your daily rhythm? Many people discover that worship becomes especially meaningful during times when they feel overwhelmed or uncertain. By choosing worship during those moments, the heart reconnects with the peace and strength that God provides.

Pause and Reflect

• When was the last time I intentionally spent time worshiping God?
• How does worship affect my perspective during difficult seasons?
• What simple ways could I include worship in my daily life?
• How might my outlook change if worship became part of my regular routine?

Prayer

Lord, help me remember that worship reconnects my heart with your presence. When life feels overwhelming, teach me to turn my attention toward your goodness and faithfulness. Fill my heart with gratitude and help me experience the peace that comes from honoring you. May my life become an expression of worship each day. Amen.

Chapter 12
The Power of Scripture

God's Word has the ability to bring light, clarity, and strength to the human soul. Throughout history, people have searched for guidance when life feels uncertain. In moments of confusion, discouragement, or important decisions, the human heart longs for direction that is trustworthy and enduring.

Many voices offer advice in the world today—friends, books, media, and personal opinions. While these sources may sometimes provide helpful insights, human wisdom is limited and often influenced by circumstances and emotions. Scripture offers something far greater.

The Bible has guided countless people across generations, cultures, and nations because it speaks not only to the mind but also to the soul. God's Word provides wisdom, correction, encouragement, and hope for those who seek its guidance.

When a person begins to engage deeply with Scripture, they discover that the Word of God does more than inform—it transforms.

Scripture Illuminates the Path

One of the most beautiful descriptions of God's Word appears in the book of Psalms: *"Your word is a lamp to my feet and a light to my path."* — Psalm 119:105

This verse paints a powerful image. Imagine walking through a dark path at night. Without light, every step becomes uncertain. Obstacles are difficult to see, and it becomes easy to lose direction.

A lamp changes everything. It may not illuminate the entire road ahead, but it provides enough light to take the next step safely. In the same way, Scripture provides guidance for life's journey. God's Word may not reveal every detail of the future at once, but it gives the wisdom necessary to move forward with confidence. Step by step, it lights the path.

Scripture Refreshes the Soul

Beyond guidance, Scripture also renews and strengthens the inner life. *"The law of the Lord is perfect, refreshing the soul. The statutes of the Lord are trustworthy, making wise the simple."* — Psalm 19:7

Life can sometimes drain emotional and spiritual energy. Disappointments, stress, and uncertainty may leave the soul feeling weary.

When people spend time reflecting on God's Word, something remarkable happens. Scripture has the ability to restore hope and bring renewed strength to the heart. It reminds readers that their lives are part of a larger story—one guided by a faithful and loving God.

Scripture Strengthens Faith

Faith grows when people encounter God's promises and truth repeatedly. *"So then faith comes by hearing, and hearing by the word of God."* — Romans 10:17

Every time someone reads or hears Scripture, their perspective begins to shift. Instead of focusing only on visible circumstances, they begin remembering the character and faithfulness of God.

Faith does not grow from wishful thinking. It grows from continually encountering God's Word.
The more truth fills the mind, the stronger faith becomes.

Scripture Teaches and Corrects

The Bible is not only a source of encouragement; it also teaches and corrects. *"All Scripture is God-breathed and is useful for teaching, rebuking, correcting and training in righteousness."* — 2 Timothy 3:16

This verse reminds us that Scripture plays many roles in the life of a believer. It teaches wisdom. It corrects harmful thinking. It guides people toward integrity and righteousness. Just as a wise mentor helps shape someone's character, God's Word shapes the life of those who engage with it regularly.

Scripture Guards the Heart

One of the most powerful ways Scripture strengthens a person is by shaping the thoughts within the heart. *"I have hidden your word in my heart that I might not sin against you."* — Psalm 119:11

When God's Word becomes part of a person's thinking, it influences how they respond to life. Instead of reacting impulsively to situations, the mind becomes anchored in truth. Words of wisdom begin guiding decisions, attitudes, and actions. The heart becomes guarded by the presence of God's Word.

Scripture Renews the Mind

Many struggles begin with the way people think about themselves, their circumstances, or their future. Scripture offers a path to renewing those patterns of thought. *"Do not conform to the pattern of this world, but be transformed by the renewing of your mind."* — Romans 12:2

Transformation begins when the mind encounters truth repeatedly. As God's Word fills the mind, discouraging or harmful thought patterns begin losing their power. Over time, the mind becomes strengthened by truth rather than overwhelmed by fear or negativity.

Scripture Reveals Truth

Another remarkable aspect of Scripture is its ability to reveal truth about both God and the human heart. *"Then you will know the truth, and the truth will set you free."* — John 8:32

Truth has the power to bring freedom. When people understand God's promises and His perspective on life, they become less controlled by fear, confusion, or discouragement. Truth creates clarity. And clarity often leads to freedom.

Scripture Discerns the Heart

The Bible describes God's Word as living and active. *"For the word of God is alive and active. Sharper than any double-edged sword."* — Hebrews 4:12

Unlike ordinary words, Scripture has the ability to reach deeply into the thoughts and motives of the heart. Sometimes a single verse can reveal something that had previously gone unnoticed—a hidden fear, an unhealthy pattern of thinking, or an area that needs healing. Yet Scripture reveals these things not to condemn but to guide the heart toward growth and restoration.

Scripture Brings Courage and Hope

God's Word often speaks courage into moments of fear or uncertainty. *"Have I not commanded you? Be strong and courageous. Do not be afraid; do not be discouraged, for the Lord your God will be with you wherever you go."* —Joshua 1:9

Verses like this remind readers that they are not alone in life's challenges. Scripture continually reassures people that God's presence accompanies them wherever they go. This assurance builds courage and hope for the future.

Scripture Nourishes the Soul

Jesus Himself described Scripture as essential spiritual nourishment. *"Man shall not live on bread alone, but on every word that comes from the mouth of God."* — Matthew 4:4

Just as the body requires food for strength, the soul requires truth for spiritual health. Regular engagement with God's Word nourishes faith, wisdom, and endurance for the journey of life.

Truth to Remember

God's Word is not merely information—it is transformation. When people read Scripture with open hearts, they discover guidance for decisions, strength for challenges, and hope for the future. God's Word illuminates the path, renews the mind, strengthens faith, and restores the soul.

Guided Reflection

Take a moment to consider your relationship with Scripture. Do you approach the Bible occasionally during difficult moments, or has it become a regular source of wisdom in your life?

Many people discover that even a few minutes each day reflecting on Scripture can gradually reshape their perspective and strengthen their faith.

Pause and Reflect

• How often do I make time to read or reflect on Scripture?

• What passages have brought encouragement during difficult seasons?

• How might my thinking change if I allowed God's Word to shape my perspective more consistently?

• What is one verse I can carry with me throughout the day?

Prayer

Lord, thank you for giving us your Word as a source of wisdom and guidance. Help me approach Scripture with humility and openness. Allow your truth to renew my mind, strengthen my heart, and guide my decisions. May your Word continue to bring light to my path and hope to my soul. Amen.

Chapter 13
The Strength of Community

Life's journey was never meant to be walked alone. Every person experiences seasons of joy, growth, uncertainty, and challenge. During these moments, one of the greatest sources of strength often comes from the people who walk alongside us. Encouragement, understanding, and shared faith can bring renewed hope when life feels difficult.

Community strengthens the soul because it reminds us that our struggles do not have to be carried alone. When people gather together in support, prayer, and encouragement, they help each other remain strong even during the most challenging seasons of life.

Why Community Matters

Human beings were created with a deep need for connection. Healthy relationships allow people to share their experiences, learn from one another, and support each other during difficult moments. When someone faces hardship without encouragement, discouragement can grow quickly. But when people stand together, something powerful happens. Hope grows stronger. Faith becomes more resilient. Burdens feel lighter.

The Bible repeatedly emphasizes the importance of fellowship and mutual encouragement. *"And let us consider how we may spur one another on toward love and good deeds, not giving up meeting together, but encouraging one another."* — Hebrews 10:24–25

Encouragement becomes contagious in healthy community. One person's faith can uplift another who may be struggling.

A Powerful Example from the Early Church

One of the most powerful demonstrations of community in Scripture appears in the story of Peter in the book of Acts. Peter had been arrested and placed in prison because of his faith. The situation appeared serious, and it was uncertain what might happen to him next.

But the believers did not respond with fear or discouragement. Instead, they gathered together and prayed. *"So Peter was kept in prison, but the church was earnestly praying to God for him."* — Acts 12:5

While Peter remained behind prison walls, the community of believers stood together in prayer. That night something extraordinary happened.

"Suddenly an angel of the Lord appeared, and a light shone in the cell. He struck Peter on the side and woke him up. 'Quick, get up!' he said, and the chains fell off Peter's wrists." — Acts 12:7

The angel led Peter past the guards and through the prison gates until he found himself standing outside in freedom. When Peter arrived at the home where the believers were gathered in prayer, they were amazed to see that God had answered their prayers.

This story reveals something powerful about community. When people stand together in faith, encouragement, and prayer, they strengthen one another in ways that would be impossible alone.

Carrying One Another's Burdens

One of the most beautiful aspects of community is the ability to support one another during difficult seasons. The Bible describes this responsibility clearly: *"Carry each other's burdens, and in this way you will fulfill the law of Christ."* — Galatians 6:2

There are moments in life when someone may feel overwhelmed by the weight of their circumstances. During those times, the presence of supportive friends, family members, or spiritual mentors can make a profound difference.

Sometimes encouragement comes through listening. Sometimes it comes through prayer. Sometimes it comes simply through being present. Even small acts of kindness can bring comfort to someone who feels discouraged.

Wisdom Found in Relationships

Community also provides wisdom. No single person has all the answers for every situation in life. But when people share their experiences and insights, they help one another grow. Scripture describes this beautifully: *"As iron sharpens iron, so one person sharpens another."* — Proverbs 27:17

Healthy relationships challenge us to grow in wisdom and maturity. Friends who speak with honesty and compassion help us see perspectives we might not recognize on our own. In this way, community becomes a place of learning and growth.

The Early Church Model

The early church understood the importance of community. Believers regularly gathered together to support one another, learn together, and grow in faith.

Scripture describes their unity: *"They devoted themselves to the apostles' teaching and to fellowship, to the breaking of bread and to prayer."* — Acts 2:42

Their gatherings strengthened their faith and created an environment where encouragement and spiritual growth flourished. This model continues to inspire communities of faith today.

Choosing Healthy Community

While community is valuable, it is important to surround ourselves with relationships that encourage growth rather than negativity. Healthy community should uplift and inspire. It should encourage faith, integrity, kindness, and wisdom.

When people spend time with others who pursue these values, their own lives are strengthened. Positive community becomes a place where individuals support each other in becoming their best selves.

Truth to Remember

Community strengthens the soul and reminds us that we are not meant to face life alone. Encouragement from others can bring hope during difficult seasons and joy during moments of celebration. When people walk together in faith and support, they often discover strength far greater than what they could achieve alone.

Guided Reflection

Take a moment to reflect on the relationships in your life. Are there people who encourage and support you during difficult seasons?

Strong community grows when people invest time, care, and honesty into their relationships. Just as others may strengthen you, you also have the ability to bring encouragement to those around you.

Pause and Reflect

• Who in my life provides encouragement and support during difficult moments?

• Am I open to sharing my struggles with trusted friends or mentors?

• How can I strengthen my relationships with people who encourage growth and faith?

• In what ways can I offer encouragement to someone else today?

Prayer

Lord, thank you for the gift of community and supportive relationships. Help me build connections that encourage faith, wisdom, and compassion. Teach me to support others during difficult seasons and to receive encouragement with humility. May the relationships in my life reflect your love and bring strength to those around me. Amen.

Chapter 14
Listening to the Guidance of the Holy Spirit

God does not leave people to navigate life alone. Through the Holy Spirit, He continues to guide, teach, and direct those who seek Him.

Life often presents situations where the right path forward is not immediately clear. Decisions about relationships, work, opportunities, or personal growth can sometimes feel overwhelming. In those moments, many people search for wisdom from different sources—friends, mentors, books, or personal experience. While these sources can offer valuable insight, believers also have access to a deeper and more reliable source of guidance. The Holy Spirit.

The Holy Spirit is described in Scripture as a helper, teacher, and guide who leads believers into truth and wisdom. Listening to the guidance of the Holy Spirit allows people to move forward with clarity and confidence even when circumstances appear uncertain.

The Role of the Holy Spirit

Jesus spoke clearly about the role of the Holy Spirit when preparing His disciples for the future. *"But the Helper, the Holy Spirit, whom the Father will send in my name, will teach you all things and remind you of everything I have said to you."* —John 14:26

This promise revealed that the disciples would not be left alone after Jesus' earthly ministry. The Holy Spirit would continue guiding them, reminding them of truth, and helping them live out what they had learned.

Another promise appears in the Gospel of John: *"But when he, the Spirit of truth, comes, he will guide you into all the truth."* —John 16:13

These words reveal that the Holy Spirit works within the hearts of believers to bring wisdom, understanding, and spiritual insight. Today, believers continue to experience this same guidance.
The Holy Spirit often works quietly within the heart, helping people recognize truth, discern wisdom, and respond with integrity.

Learning to Recognize God's Guidance

Many people wonder how they can recognize the guidance of the Holy Spirit. Often God's direction does not appear through dramatic signs or sudden revelations. Instead, it frequently comes through quiet conviction, gentle prompting, and inner clarity. The Holy Spirit may prompt someone toward patience when they feel tempted to respond with anger. He may encourage forgiveness when resentment begins growing in the heart. He may guide someone toward a decision that reflects wisdom and integrity.

These moments of inner awareness become clearer when people spend time in prayer and Scripture. As the heart becomes more attentive to God, the voice of the Holy Spirit becomes easier to recognize. Scripture reminds believers: *"For those who are led by the Spirit of God are the children of God."* — Romans 8:14

Being led by the Spirit is part of the spiritual journey of every believer.

A Biblical Example of Guidance

The early church experienced the guidance of the Holy Spirit in remarkable ways. In the book of Acts, we see how believers relied on the Spirit's direction as they carried out their mission. One moment that illustrates this appears during the ministry of Philip.

"The Spirit told Philip, 'Go to that chariot and stay near it.'"
— Acts 8:29

Philip obeyed the guidance he sensed, and this simple act of obedience led him to meet an Ethiopian official who was seeking understanding of Scripture. Through that encounter, Philip explained the message of faith, and the man responded with belief and was baptized. What began as a quiet prompting from the Holy Spirit became a moment that changed someone's life.

This story reminds us that when people listen to God's guidance, their obedience can impact others in meaningful ways.

The Importance of Obedience

Guidance becomes meaningful when it is followed by action. Throughout Scripture, individuals who experienced God's direction responded with obedience.

Obedience does not always mean the path will be easy. Sometimes following God's guidance requires courage and trust. Yet obedience often leads to growth, clarity, and purpose.

When people consistently respond to the gentle prompting of the Holy Spirit, their lives begin aligning more closely with God's direction. Scripture encourages believers to remain attentive to this guidance: *"Since we live by the Spirit, let us keep in step with the Spirit."* — Galatians 5:25

Walking in step with the Spirit means allowing God's guidance to shape daily decisions and attitudes.

Peace as Confirmation

Another way people sometimes recognize God's guidance is through the presence of peace. When a decision aligns with wisdom and truth, the heart often experiences a sense of calm assurance even if the circumstances remain uncertain. Scripture reflects this idea: *"Let the peace of Christ rule in your hearts."* — Colossians 3:15

Peace does not necessarily remove every challenge, but it provides confidence that the chosen direction aligns with God's guidance. This inner peace often becomes a valuable indicator when discerning important decisions.

Growing in Spiritual Awareness

Learning to recognize the Holy Spirit's guidance is a process that develops over time. As people regularly spend time in prayer, Scripture, and reflection, their sensitivity to God's direction increases. They begin noticing moments when wisdom rises within them, guiding their responses and decisions. Gradually their lives become shaped by a deeper awareness of God's presence. Over time they learn that God often guides through quiet wisdom rather than dramatic signs.

Truth to Remember

The Holy Spirit guides those who seek God with sincerity and humility. When people pause to listen, reflect, and seek wisdom, they often discover that God provides guidance through Scripture, prayer, wise counsel, and inner peace. This guidance helps shape decisions that align with faith, integrity, and purpose.

Guided Reflection

Consider the decisions and situations you are currently facing. Have there been moments when you sensed a gentle prompting toward wisdom, patience, or a particular direction? Often the guidance of the Holy Spirit becomes clearer when we slow down, pray, and seek God's perspective. Learning to listen creates space for that guidance to become more visible.

Pause and Reflect

• When making important decisions, do I pause to seek God's guidance?

• Have there been moments when I sensed a quiet prompting toward wisdom or patience?

• How can I create more space in my daily life to listen for God's direction?

• What step of obedience might God be encouraging me to take?

Prayer

Lord, thank you for giving us the Holy Spirit to guide and teach us. Help me learn to recognize your direction in my life. Give me wisdom when making decisions and courage to follow your guidance. May my heart remain open to your voice as I walk forward in faith. Amen.

PART III

Walking in Renewal and Purpose

Living with faith, compassion, and strength as a new chapter begins

Understanding the struggles of the soul and learning the spiritual practices that restore it are important steps in the journey of transformation. Yet the journey does not end there.

When healing begins and strength is restored, life opens into a new season. This season is not only about overcoming past struggles but also about walking forward with renewed purpose and clarity. A restored soul begins to see life differently. Challenges are approached with greater wisdom. Relationships are nurtured with greater compassion. Opportunities are embraced with renewed courage. God's work in a person's life does not stop at restoration—it continues through growth, purpose, and service to others.

In this final section, we will explore how renewed hearts begin to live differently. Gratitude, compassion, faithfulness, and wise words become part of daily life. These qualities strengthen the soul and influence the world around us.

When people walk in spiritual strength, their lives often become a source of encouragement to others. The journey of renewal becomes a journey of purpose.

Chapter 15
The Power of Gratitude

Gratitude has the ability to transform the way we see life. Many people naturally express gratitude when life is going well. When circumstances are pleasant and blessings are obvious, it feels easy to say "thank you." But gratitude becomes especially powerful during seasons when life feels uncertain or difficult. In those moments, gratitude does something remarkable. It shifts the focus of the heart away from what is lacking and toward what is already present.

Instead of allowing discouragement to dominate our thoughts, gratitude reminds us of the many ways God continues to work in our lives. This shift in perspective can bring renewed strength and hope.

Gratitude Changes Perspective

Life often contains both challenges and blessings at the same time. Yet human nature sometimes causes people to focus primarily on the difficulties they are facing. When problems occupy most of our attention, it becomes easy to overlook the many ways God has already provided, protected, and guided us. Gratitude changes this perspective.

When people intentionally acknowledge the good things in their lives—both large and small—they begin recognizing that God's faithfulness has been present all along. Gratitude does not deny the presence of challenges, but it refuses to allow those challenges to overshadow every blessing.

A Biblical Encouragement Toward Gratitude

The Bible encourages believers to cultivate gratitude as a consistent attitude of the heart. *"Give thanks in all circumstances; for this is God's will for you in Christ Jesus."* — 1 Thessalonians 5:18

This verse does not say to give thanks **for every circumstance**, but rather **in every circumstance**. In other words, gratitude can exist even when life is not perfect.

Even during difficult seasons, there are still reasons to be thankful—moments of kindness, opportunities for growth, and reminders of God's presence. Choosing gratitude in these moments strengthens faith and renews hope.

A Real-Life Scenario

Imagine someone facing a difficult period in their life. Perhaps they are navigating financial uncertainty, emotional stress, or unexpected change. At first their thoughts may revolve around everything that feels uncertain. But then they begin intentionally practicing gratitude. They start noticing small blessings they previously overlooked—the support of a friend, the beauty of a quiet morning, the strength they have gained through previous challenges.

Gradually their perspective begins to shift. The difficulties may still exist, but they no longer define the entire picture. Gratitude allows hope to grow again.

The Example of Jesus Giving Thanks

Even in moments of great responsibility and challenge, Jesus demonstrated gratitude. Before performing the miracle of feeding the large crowd with a small amount of food, Scripture records that Jesus first gave thanks. *"Taking the five loaves and the two fish and looking up to heaven, he gave thanks and broke the loaves."* — Matthew 14:19

This moment reveals something important. Gratitude often precedes breakthrough. Before the miracle multiplied the food, gratitude was already present.

This example reminds us that gratitude can open the heart to recognize God's provision even before the outcome becomes visible.

Gratitude Strengthens the Heart

When gratitude becomes a regular practice, it gradually strengthens the inner life. People who cultivate gratitude often experience greater peace and resilience during challenging moments. Instead of becoming overwhelmed by every difficulty, they develop the ability to remember that God's faithfulness has carried them through many seasons before. Scripture expresses this idea beautifully:

"Enter his gates with thanksgiving and his courts with praise; give thanks to him and praise his name." — Psalm 100:4

Gratitude draws the heart closer to God and reminds us of His goodness.

Gratitude as a Daily Practice

Gratitude does not need to be limited to special occasions. It can become part of everyday life. Some people begin their day by thanking God for the gift of a new morning. Others reflect on moments of blessing before going to sleep at night.

These simple practices gradually train the heart to recognize goodness more easily. Over time, gratitude becomes a habit that shapes how a person views life.

The Example of the Ten Healed Men

The Bible provides a powerful story that highlights the importance of gratitude. One day, ten men suffering from leprosy approached Jesus. At that time, leprosy was a disease that often forced people to live separated from society. Those who had it were considered unclean and were isolated from their families and communities.

The men called out to Jesus, asking Him for mercy. Jesus responded by instructing them to go and show themselves to the priests. As they obeyed His instruction and went on their way, something remarkable happened. They were healed. Scripture records the moment: *"As they went, they were cleansed."* — Luke 17:14

Ten people received the same miracle. Yet only one returned. *"One of them, when he saw he was healed, came back, praising God in a loud voice."* — Luke 17:15

The man who returned fell at Jesus' feet and thanked Him. He recognized not only the miracle he had received but also the one who had given it.

Jesus then asked an important question: *"Were not all ten cleansed? Where are the other nine?"* — Luke 17:17

This moment reveals a powerful truth. Many people receive blessings, but fewer pause to express gratitude. Gratitude acknowledges the source of the blessing. It recognizes that what we have received is not something to take for granted.

The one man who returned experienced something deeper than physical healing—he demonstrated a heart that recognized the goodness of God.

This story reminds us that gratitude is not only about saying thank you. It is about recognizing and honoring the source of every blessing.

Truth to Remember

Gratitude shifts the heart from discouragement toward hope. When people intentionally recognize God's goodness—even in small ways—they begin discovering renewed strength and perspective. Gratitude does not remove life's challenges, but it reminds the heart that blessings continue to exist alongside them.

Guided Reflection

Take a moment to reflect on the role gratitude plays in your life. Are there blessings you may have overlooked during busy or difficult seasons? Sometimes pausing to recognize even the smallest gifts can restore hope and strengthen faith. Gratitude opens the eyes to see that God's presence has been with us all along.

Pause and Reflect

• What are three things I can thank God for today?
• Have there been moments when gratitude changed my perspective during a difficult season?
• How can I make gratitude a more regular part of my daily life?
• Who in my life could benefit from hearing words of gratitude or encouragement?

Prayer

Lord, thank you for the many ways you provide, guide, and strengthen my life. Help me develop a grateful heart that recognizes your goodness even during difficult seasons. Teach me to focus on the blessings you have placed in my life and to carry gratitude with me each day. Amen.

Chapter 16
Helping Others and Living with Compassion

One of the greatest signs of a healed heart is the ability to care about the needs of others. When people go through difficult seasons, their attention often turns inward. Pain, uncertainty, and struggle can consume a person's thoughts and emotions. During those times, survival and healing become the primary focus. This is natural.

But something beautiful begins to happen as healing takes place. As the heart becomes stronger, it gradually shifts from focusing only on personal struggles to noticing the needs of others. Compassion begins to grow.

People who have experienced hardship often develop a deeper understanding of the struggles others face. Their experiences allow them to offer encouragement, kindness, and support in ways that feel genuine and meaningful. In this way, personal healing often becomes the foundation for helping others.

Compassion Reflects the Heart of God

Throughout Scripture, compassion appears as a central characteristic of God's nature. Jesus repeatedly demonstrated compassion toward people who were hurting, discouraged, or overlooked by society. One passage describes this beautifully:

"When he saw the crowds, he had compassion on them, because they were harassed and helpless, like sheep without a shepherd."
— Matthew 9:36

Jesus did not ignore the struggles of those around Him. Instead, He responded with care, understanding, and action. Another moment reveals the same heart of compassion: *"Jesus wept."* —John 11:35

Even though Jesus knew that Lazarus would soon be raised from the dead, He still responded to the grief of those around Him with deep compassion. These moments remind us that compassion is not weakness. It is a reflection of God's own heart.

A Simple Act Can Change Someone's Day

Helping others does not always require extraordinary gestures. Often the most meaningful acts of compassion are simple.

Listening to someone who needs encouragement. Offering support during a difficult moment. Providing practical help when someone is struggling. Speaking words of hope to someone who feels discouraged.

These small actions can bring comfort and hope to people who may feel unseen or overwhelmed. Sometimes a single act of kindness can remind someone that they are not alone.

Scripture encourages this kind of generosity: *"Therefore encourage one another and build each other up."* — 1 Thessalonians 5:11

Encouragement has the power to strengthen hearts in ways we may never fully realize.

The Example of the Good Samaritan

Jesus once told a story that beautifully illustrates compassion in action. In the parable of the Good Samaritan, a man was traveling along a road when he was attacked and left injured. Several people passed by him without stopping to help. Eventually, a Samaritan traveler saw the injured man and responded with compassion.

"But a Samaritan, as he traveled, came where the man was; and when he saw him, he took pity on him." — Luke 10:33

The Samaritan did not ignore the situation or assume someone else would help. Instead, he cared for the injured man, treated his wounds, and ensured he received further care.

This story reminds readers that compassion often requires action. Helping others sometimes means stepping outside of our routines to meet someone's need.

Compassion Strengthens Community

When people practice compassion, they contribute to stronger and healthier communities. Acts of kindness encourage trust, connection, and mutual support. People begin to feel valued and cared for.

In many ways, compassion creates a ripple effect. One act of kindness often inspires another. Encouragement spreads from one person to the next. The world becomes brighter when people choose to care for one another. Scripture reminds believers of this calling: *"Carry each other's burdens, and in this way you will fulfill the law of Christ."* — Galatians 6:2

Helping others allows people to experience the strength of shared support.

Compassion as a Way of Life

Living with compassion means developing a mindset that remains attentive to the needs of others. Scripture encourages believers to cultivate this attitude: *"Be kind and compassionate to one another, forgiving each other, just as in Christ God forgave you."* — Ephesians 4:32

This verse reminds readers that compassion flows from a heart that understands grace. When people remember the kindness and mercy they have received from God, they often feel inspired to extend that same kindness to others. Over time, compassion becomes more than an occasional act—it becomes a way of life.

Truth to Remember

A healed heart naturally becomes a compassionate heart. When people experience healing, encouragement, and grace in their own lives, they often feel motivated to share that same compassion with others. Helping someone else may seem like a small action, but it can have a profound impact. Kindness has the power to restore hope.

Guided Reflection

Take a moment to consider the ways compassion appears in your life. Have you experienced moments when someone's kindness brought encouragement during a difficult season? Those experiences often inspire us to extend the same care to others. Helping someone else does not require perfection. It simply requires a willing heart.

Pause and Reflect

• Who in my life might need encouragement right now?

• How can I show compassion through simple acts of kindness?

• Have I experienced moments when someone's kindness made a difference in my life?

• How can I make compassion a regular part of my daily life?

Prayer

Lord, thank you for the compassion you have shown toward me. Help me develop a heart that notices the needs of others. Teach me to respond with kindness, patience, and generosity. May my actions reflect your love and bring encouragement to those around me. Amen.

Chapter 17
Faithfulness in the Small Things

Great transformation often begins with small, consistent acts of faithfulness. Many people desire significant change in their lives. They hope for breakthroughs, opportunities, and moments that dramatically alter their circumstances.

While these moments can certainly occur, lasting growth is often built through something much simpler—faithfulness in the small things. Daily choices, quiet acts of obedience, and consistent discipline gradually shape a person's character and direction. Small steps may seem insignificant at first, but over time they create meaningful progress.

The Power of Small Decisions

Life is made up of countless small decisions. Choosing to speak kindly when frustration arises. Choosing patience when circumstances feel difficult. Choosing integrity when shortcuts appear tempting. Choosing perseverance when the journey feels long. Each of these decisions may feel minor in the moment, yet together they form the foundation of a person's character.

Faithfulness in these small areas builds trust, wisdom, and resilience. Over time, these qualities prepare individuals for greater responsibilities and opportunities.

A Teaching from Jesus

Jesus once emphasized the importance of faithfulness in small matters. *"Whoever can be trusted with very little can also be trusted with much."* — Luke 16:10

This teaching reveals an important principle. Faithfulness is not measured only by large accomplishments. It is demonstrated through the consistent way someone handles ordinary responsibilities. When people show integrity in small situations, they develop habits that strengthen them for larger challenges.

A Real-Life Scenario

Consider someone who desires a meaningful change in their life. Perhaps they want to strengthen their spiritual life, improve their relationships, or pursue a new goal. At first the path may feel overwhelming because the desired outcome appears far away. But progress often begins with simple steps.

Setting aside a few moments each day for reflection or prayer. Practicing gratitude regularly. Showing patience in conversations. Choosing encouragement instead of criticism.

Over time these small practices accumulate, gradually shaping a new pattern of life. The transformation may not happen overnight, but it becomes visible through steady progress.

Faithfulness Builds Character

Character is rarely formed through dramatic moments alone. Instead, it grows through repeated choices that reflect integrity and perseverance. Scripture encourages believers to remain steady and faithful in their actions. *"Whatever you do, work at it with all your heart, as working for the Lord."* — Colossians 3:23

This verse reminds readers that even the most ordinary tasks can carry meaning when approached with dedication and sincerity. Faithfulness in everyday responsibilities reflects a heart that seeks to honor God through consistent effort.

The Parable of the Talents

Jesus illustrated the value of faithfulness through a well-known parable. In this story, a master entrusted different amounts of resources to his servants before leaving on a journey. Some servants used what they were given wisely, investing their resources and producing growth.

When the master returned, he praised their faithfulness. *"Well done, good and faithful servant! You have been faithful with a few things; I will put you in charge of many things."* — Matthew 25:21

The message of this story is clear. Faithfulness with what we have today prepares us for greater opportunities tomorrow.

Growth Happens Gradually

In a world that often celebrates quick success, it can be easy to overlook the importance of gradual growth. But many of life's most meaningful achievements develop slowly.

Relationships deepen through consistent care. Skills improve through practice. Wisdom grows through experience. Spiritual maturity develops through daily faithfulness. Scripture reminds us that even small beginnings can lead to greater outcomes. *"Do not despise these small beginnings, for the Lord rejoices to see the work begin."* — Zechariah 4:10

When people remain committed to small acts of integrity and perseverance, they build a foundation that supports lasting progress.

Truth to Remember

Faithfulness in small things prepares the way for greater growth. When people commit themselves to consistent integrity and dedication, they develop the strength and character necessary for the opportunities that lie ahead. Small steps taken faithfully can lead to remarkable transformation over time.

Guided Reflection

Consider the small responsibilities and opportunities present in your life right now. Sometimes the path toward meaningful change begins by approaching these daily moments with renewed faithfulness and care. Even simple actions, repeated consistently, can shape the future in powerful ways.

Pause and Reflect

- What small areas of my life require greater faithfulness or consistency?
- Are there daily habits that could strengthen my spiritual or personal growth?
- How might small acts of integrity shape my future opportunities?

• What step of faithfulness can I begin practicing today?

Prayer

Lord, help me remain faithful in the small responsibilities of daily life. Teach me to approach each task with integrity, patience, and dedication. Give me the strength to remain consistent even when progress feels slow. May my faithfulness today prepare me for the opportunities you have ahead. Amen.

Chapter 18
Guarding Your Words and Confessions

Words have the power to shape thoughts, influence emotions, and guide the direction of life. Every day people speak thousands of words. Some are spoken casually in conversation, while others express deeper beliefs about life, circumstances, and personal identity.

What many people do not immediately realize is that words often reflect the condition of the heart and the patterns of the mind. The way someone speaks about their life, their future, and their challenges can gradually influence how they experience those realities.

Words can build hope or reinforce discouragement. They can encourage growth or deepen fear. Learning to guard our words and speak with wisdom is therefore an important step toward spiritual and emotional strength.

The Influence of Words

Words carry influence far beyond the moment they are spoken. When someone repeatedly speaks negatively about their abilities or future, those statements can slowly shape how they see themselves. Over time those thoughts may affect decisions, confidence, and expectations.

On the other hand, words that reflect truth, hope, and faith can strengthen the mind and encourage perseverance. Scripture acknowledges the power of words clearly: *"The tongue has the power of life and death, and those who love it will eat its fruit."* — Proverbs 18:21

This verse reminds us that words can either bring life and encouragement or reinforce discouragement and negativity. Choosing words wisely helps guide the heart toward hope rather than fear.

Words Reflect the Heart

The words people speak often reveal what is happening inside the heart. Jesus described this connection when speaking about the relationship between thoughts and speech. *"For the mouth speaks what the heart is full of."* — Matthew 12:34

When the heart is filled with discouragement or fear, those emotions may appear in speech. But when the heart becomes filled with truth, gratitude, and faith, those qualities also begin to shape the words people use.

Guarding our words therefore begins with guarding our thoughts and attitudes. Scripture encourages believers to nurture a healthy mindset: *"Let the words of my mouth and the meditation of my heart be pleasing in your sight, Lord."* — Psalm 19:14

When both our thoughts and words align with truth, our lives become more grounded in wisdom and peace.

A Real-Life Scenario

Imagine someone going through a challenging season in their life. They may begin saying things such as: "I will never overcome this." "Nothing ever works out for me." "There is no point in trying."

Although these statements may express genuine frustration, repeating them frequently can strengthen discouragement rather than resolve it.

Now imagine the same person gradually learning to speak differently: "This season is difficult, but it will not last forever." "I am learning and growing through this experience." "I will continue moving forward."

The circumstances may remain the same, but the shift in language begins shaping a different outlook. Words influence the direction of the mind.

Speaking Words That Build Faith

The Bible encourages believers to speak words that strengthen and encourage both themselves and others. *"Do not let any unwholesome talk come out of your mouths, but only what is helpful for building others up according to their needs."* — Ephesians 4:29

This verse reminds readers that speech should reflect wisdom and kindness. Words can encourage someone who feels discouraged. They can bring comfort during moments of uncertainty.

When people intentionally choose words that uplift and strengthen others, they contribute to an environment of encouragement and hope.

The Example of Faith-Filled Speech

Throughout Scripture we see examples of individuals who chose to speak with faith even during uncertain circumstances. One powerful example appears in the life of David.

Before facing the giant Goliath, David spoke confidently about God's ability to deliver him. *"The Lord who rescued me from the paw of the lion and the paw of the bear will rescue me from the hand of this Philistine."* — 1 Samuel 17:37

David's words reflected trust rather than fear. His confidence did not come from his own strength but from his faith in God's faithfulness. This example reminds readers that words spoken with faith can strengthen courage during difficult moments.

Practicing Wise Speech

Guarding our words does not mean ignoring difficulties or pretending that challenges do not exist. Instead, it means choosing language that reflects truth, wisdom, and hope rather than allowing discouragement to dominate our speech. This practice often begins with small changes.

- Pausing before speaking during moments of frustration.
- Replacing negative assumptions with thoughtful reflection.
- Speaking encouragement to others.
- Choosing gratitude rather than complaint.

These habits gradually reshape both speech and mindset. Over time, wise speech becomes a reflection of a transformed heart.

Truth to Remember

Words shape the atmosphere of the heart and influence the direction of life. When people choose words that reflect truth, encouragement, and faith, they strengthen both themselves and those around them. Guarding our words is therefore an important step toward living with wisdom, confidence, and hope.

Guided Reflection

Take a moment to consider the words you most frequently speak about your life and circumstances. Do your words reflect discouragement, or do they express hope and faith? Becoming aware of how we speak allows us to choose words that align with truth and encourage growth.

Pause and Reflect

• What types of words do I most often speak about my life and circumstances?
• Are there patterns of speech that may reinforce discouragement?

• How can I begin using words that bring encouragement and hope?
• In what ways can my words strengthen someone else today?

Prayer

Lord, help me guard my words and speak with wisdom. Teach me to use language that reflects truth, encouragement, and faith. When I feel tempted to speak in frustration or discouragement, remind me to pause and seek your guidance. May my words bring life and encouragement to those around me. Amen.

Chapter 19
Walking in Spiritual Strength

Spiritual strength is not built in a single moment. It grows through daily commitment, faith, and trust in God.

Throughout this book, we have explored many of the struggles that affect the human soul—feelings of rejection, discouragement, comparison, negative thinking, and isolation. These experiences are part of life's journey, and many people encounter them at different seasons.

Yet the purpose of this journey has not been simply to identify these struggles. The purpose has been transformation.

Healing begins when people recognize the battles they face, but true growth happens when they begin living differently—strengthened by wisdom, faith, and spiritual awareness. Walking in spiritual strength means continuing to apply the principles that bring renewal to the heart.

Strength Comes Through Daily Choices

Spiritual strength does not develop through occasional inspiration alone. Instead, it grows through daily choices that reflect faith and commitment.

Choosing prayer when life feels overwhelming. Choosing gratitude when circumstances feel uncertain. Choosing patience when frustration arises. Choosing hope when discouragement attempts to take hold.

These choices may appear small in the moment, yet over time they shape a resilient and grounded life. Just as physical strength grows through consistent exercise, spiritual strength grows through consistent practice of faith.

Strength Through God's Presence

One of the most powerful sources of spiritual strength is the awareness that God's presence remains with us through every season of life. Scripture offers this encouragement: *"God is our refuge and strength, an ever-present help in trouble."* — Psalm 46:1

This verse reminds readers that strength does not come only from personal effort. It also comes from trusting in God's presence and guidance.

Another passage offers similar reassurance: *"Those who hope in the Lord will renew their strength. They will soar on wings like eagles."* — Isaiah 40:31

When people rely on God during difficult moments, they discover a strength that goes beyond their own abilities.

A Biblical Example of Endurance

The apostle Paul experienced many challenges throughout his life—imprisonment, hardship, and opposition. Yet he continued moving forward with remarkable perseverance.

Paul understood that his strength did not depend solely on his circumstances. Instead, he trusted the strength that God provided. *"I can do all things through Christ who strengthens me."* — Philippians 4:13

This verse reflects a mindset that recognizes the partnership between human effort and divine support.

Paul did not claim that life would always be easy. Rather, he acknowledged that God's strength enabled him to continue faithfully regardless of circumstances.

Guarding the Progress You Have Made

As people grow spiritually and emotionally, it becomes important to protect that growth. Old habits of thinking may occasionally try to return. Moments of discouragement may arise unexpectedly. During those times, it is helpful to remember the lessons learned along the journey.

Returning to prayer. Reflecting on Scripture. Seeking encouragement from community. Practicing gratitude and wise speech.

These practices help maintain the progress that has been made. Growth becomes sustainable when people continue nurturing the habits that strengthen their faith.

Encouraging Others Along the Way

Walking in spiritual strength also allows people to encourage others who may still be navigating difficult seasons. Someone who has experienced healing and growth can often provide hope to another person who feels discouraged.

Words of encouragement, shared wisdom, or simple acts of kindness may remind others that change and healing are possible.

Scripture encourages believers to support one another in this way: *"Therefore encourage one another and build each other up."* — 1 Thessalonians 5:11

In this way, spiritual strength becomes something that benefits not only the individual but also the community around them.

Truth to Remember

Spiritual strength grows through consistent faith, trust in God, and daily commitment to wise choices. The journey of healing and growth does not end with a single moment of realization. Instead, it continues through the choices people make each day as they walk forward with renewed purpose. Each step of faith builds a stronger foundation for the future.

Guided Reflection

Take a moment to reflect on the progress you have made in your own life. What lessons from this journey have strengthened your perspective or deepened your faith? Growth often becomes visible when people look back and recognize how far they have come. Remembering those moments can provide encouragement as you continue moving forward.

Pause and Reflect

• What practices have helped strengthen my spiritual life?

• How can I continue applying these practices in my daily life?

• What progress have I made that I may not have recognized before?

• How can my experiences encourage someone else who may be struggling?

Prayer

Lord, thank you for the strength and guidance you provide each day. Help me continue walking in the wisdom and faith that I have learned. When challenges arise, remind me that your presence remains with me. Strengthen my heart so that I may continue growing and encouraging others along the journey. Amen.

Chapter 20
A New Beginning

Every journey of healing leads to a moment where the past no longer controls the future.

Throughout this book, we have explored many of the battles that can affect the human soul. Feelings of rejection, discouragement, comparison, negative thoughts, and isolation can sometimes make life feel overwhelming.

Many people carry these burdens quietly. They may wonder if their circumstances will ever change or if their struggles will always define their story. But one of the most important truths we can remember is this:

The past does not determine the future.

Healing and renewal are always possible when people choose to move forward with faith, wisdom, and trust in God. A new beginning often starts with a simple decision—to believe that change is possible.

Letting Go of What Is Behind

For many people, moving forward requires releasing the weight of past experiences. Memories of disappointment, mistakes, or painful seasons may sometimes make it difficult to see new possibilities ahead. Yet Scripture encourages believers to focus on the future rather than remaining trapped by the past. *"Forgetting what is behind and straining toward what is ahead, I press on toward the goal."* — Philippians 3:13–14

These words remind us that life continues to unfold with new opportunities. While the past may have shaped part of our story, it does not have to limit what comes next. What once felt like a closed door may simply be the beginning of a new path.

God Creates New Paths

The Bible often speaks about God's ability to bring renewal into situations that once seemed hopeless. *"See, I am doing a new thing! Now it springs up; do you not perceive it?"* — Isaiah 43:19

God specializes in new beginnings. He restores what was broken. He renews what was weakened. He brings light into places that once seemed dark.

Sometimes the new path begins quietly—through small steps of faith, moments of courage, and decisions to trust God even when the outcome is not yet visible. But over time those steps lead toward transformation.

Your Story Is Still Being Written

Every person's life is a story that continues unfolding. There may be chapters filled with challenges, uncertainty, or pain. Yet there are also chapters filled with growth, wisdom, and renewal.

The pages ahead remain unwritten. This means that the future still holds possibility. The lessons learned through difficult seasons can become the foundation for a stronger and wiser life moving forward. What once felt like a setback may later become the very story that encourages someone else. Sometimes the greatest testimonies are written in the seasons that once felt like the greatest struggles.

Living with Renewed Purpose

A new beginning is not simply about leaving the past behind. It is also about embracing a new perspective for the future. Living with renewed purpose means applying the lessons learned along the journey:

- Praying consistently

- Seeking wisdom through Scripture
- Cultivating gratitude
- Building strong community
- Walking with compassion and faithfulness

These practices strengthen the soul and help create a life guided by purpose rather than fear. Purpose grows when people walk forward with trust and obedience.

Walking Forward with Confidence

When people begin to see life through a renewed perspective, they discover that their future holds greater hope than they once imagined. Strength grows through faith. Peace grows through trust. Purpose grows through obedience and compassion.

Scripture reminds us that God walks with those who place their trust in Him. *"The Lord makes firm the steps of the one who delights in him."* — Psalm 37:23

And again we are reminded: *"For I know the plans I have for you," declares the Lord, "plans to prosper you and not to harm you, plans to give you hope and a future."* — Jeremiah 29:11

Each step forward becomes part of a journey guided by faith and strengthened by hope.

Truth to Remember

A new beginning is always possible when the heart chooses faith, hope, and trust in God. The struggles of the past do not define the future. Every day provides an opportunity to move forward with renewed strength and purpose.

Guided Reflection

Take a moment to reflect on the journey you have experienced while reading this book. Which lessons have encouraged you most? What new perspectives have begun shaping the way you see your life and your future? The answers to these questions may help guide the next steps of your journey.

Pause and Reflect

- What past experiences do I need to release in order to move forward?
- What new opportunities might God be placing before me?
- How can I apply the lessons from this journey in my daily life?
- What kind of future do I want to begin building today?

A Final Encouragement

If the journey of this book has reminded you of anything, let it be this: Your life still holds purpose. The struggles you have faced do not cancel your future. God continues to work in ways that may not always be immediately visible.

Even now, new opportunities for growth, healing, and transformation are unfolding. The next chapter of your life has not yet been written. And the steps you take today may become the beginning of a story filled with faith, courage, and renewal.

Final Prayer

Lord, thank you for the journey of healing and renewal. Help me release the weight of the past and walk forward with faith and confidence. Guide my steps as I begin this new chapter of life. Fill my heart with hope, wisdom, and courage so that I may live with purpose and bring encouragement to others. Amen.

Conclusion
Continue the Journey

The journey of life often includes moments of struggle, uncertainty, and growth. Throughout this book, we have explored many of the challenges that affect the human soul—feelings of rejection, comparison, discouragement, isolation, and negative thinking.

These experiences are not uncommon. Many people encounter them at different stages of life. At times, the weight of these struggles can make the path forward feel uncertain. Yet the purpose of this journey has been to discover an important truth:

Healing, renewal, and transformation are possible.

Winning the battle for your soul does not mean that life will never present challenges again. Instead, it means learning how to face those challenges with wisdom, faith, and resilience. It means recognizing that even in difficult seasons, growth is still possible and hope is never lost.

Throughout these pages, we have explored practices that strengthen the heart and guide the soul toward renewal. Each chapter has offered tools to help build a stronger and more resilient life:

- prayer that reconnects us with God
- worship that lifts the spirit
- Scripture that provides wisdom and direction
- community that brings encouragement and support
- gratitude that shifts our perspective
- compassion that allows us to help others
- faithfulness in daily choices that shapes our character

These practices are not simply ideas to reflect on—they are pathways that help build a life rooted in strength, faith, and purpose. Scripture reminds us of the transformation that can take place within the human heart: *"Do not conform to the pattern of this world, but be transformed by the renewing of your mind."* — Romans 12:2

Renewal begins when people choose to think differently, speak differently, and live with greater awareness of God's presence and guidance. And as we continue forward, we are reminded of another powerful promise:

"The Lord will guide you always; he will satisfy your needs and strengthen your frame." — Isaiah 58:11

This promise reminds us that we do not walk this journey alone. God continues to guide, strengthen, and renew those who seek Him.

As you continue forward from this point, remember that every new day provides another opportunity to grow, to learn, and to walk in the freedom that God desires for your life.

Growth is not always immediate, and progress may sometimes feel slow. Yet every step taken with faith and intention moves the journey forward. Your story is still unfolding. The chapters that lie ahead hold possibilities that may not yet be visible. The lessons you have learned, the strength you have gained, and the faith you continue to develop will help shape the path before you.

And as you continue this journey, may you walk with confidence, wisdom, and hope—knowing that the best chapters of your story may still be ahead.

About the Author

Racheal Odoy is a faith-based author who writes to encourage and strengthen people navigating life's challenges. Through her writing, she seeks to help readers discover healing, renewed hope, and inner strength during difficult seasons.

Her work focuses on spiritual growth, emotional resilience, and the transformative power of faith. By combining biblical principles with practical life insights, she guides readers toward a deeper understanding of themselves and a closer relationship with God.

Racheal believes that even the most difficult experiences can become opportunities for growth, restoration, and purpose. Her passion is to inspire individuals from all walks of life to overcome inner struggles and move forward with courage, wisdom, and faith.

Through her books and ministry, she hopes to remind readers that no season of life is beyond the reach of God's grace and renewal.

To learn more about Racheal Odoy, access additional resources, or stay connected with her ministry, visit:

www.rachealodoyministries.com

Stay Connected

Thank you for taking this journey through *Winning the Battle for Your Soul.*

If this book has encouraged you, consider sharing it with someone who may also benefit from its message. You are also warmly invited to stay connected for future books, teachings, and resources designed to encourage faith, healing, and personal growth.

Many readers find that continuing to learn, reflect, and grow alongside others strengthens the lessons discovered along the journey.

To stay connected and learn more about upcoming resources and ministry updates, visit:

www.rachealodoyministries.com

May the message of this book continue to encourage you as you move forward with renewed hope, strength, and faith.

A Personal Note to the Reader

Thank you for taking the time to read *Winning the Battle for Your Soul.*

If you have come this far, it means you have walked through every chapter of this journey—reflecting, learning, and perhaps recognizing parts of your own life within these pages.

Many of the struggles discussed in this book are experiences that people quietly carry in their hearts. Feelings of discouragement, comparison, rejection, or uncertainty can sometimes make the journey of life feel overwhelming.

But as you have seen throughout this book, these struggles do not have to define your story.

Healing is possible.
Growth is possible.
A new beginning is possible.

If even one chapter in this book has encouraged you, strengthened your faith, or helped you see your life with renewed hope, then its purpose has already begun to take shape.

My prayer is that the lessons within these pages will continue to guide and strengthen you long after you finish reading. May they remind you that no season of life is beyond God's ability to restore and renew. Remember that every new day offers an opportunity to move forward with wisdom, courage, and faith. Your journey continues, and the best chapters of your life may still be ahead.

With encouragement and hope,
Racheal Odoy

Share This Message

If this book has encouraged you, consider sharing it with someone who may also benefit from its message. Many people quietly struggle with the very battles discussed in these pages. A simple recommendation, meaningful conversation, or the gift of this book could bring encouragement and hope to someone who needs it.

You may also consider leaving a review where you purchased the book. Your thoughts can help other readers discover this message and begin their own journey toward healing and renewal.

Every shared message has the potential to reach another heart.

Thank you for being part of this journey.

www.ingramcontent.com/pod-product-compliance
Lightning Source LLC
LaVergne TN
LVHW010834120826
845149LV00016B/2386